DATE DUE			

202
HAC

3 24571 0900732 2
Hackney Blackwell,
Amy.

Lent, Yom Kippur,
and other atonement
days

MORRILL ES
CHICAGO PUBLIC SCHOOLS
6011 S ROCKWELL ST
CHICAGO, IL 60629

398239 03996   23432B   0001

HOLIDAYS AND CELEBRATIONS

Carnival
Christmas and Hanukkah
Easter, Passover, and Other Spring Festivals
Halloween and Commemorations of the Dead
Independence Days
Lent, Yom Kippur, and Other Atonement Days
Ramadan
Religious New Year's Celebrations
Thanksgiving and Other Harvest Festivals
Western and Chinese New Year's Celebrations

LENT, YOM KIPPUR, AND OTHER ATONEMENT DAYS

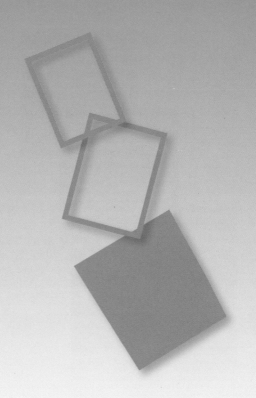

LENT, YOM KIPPUR, AND OTHER ATONEMENT DAYS

Amy
Hackney
Blackwell

CHELSEA HOUSE
PUBLISHERS
An imprint of Infobase Publishing

Lent, Yom Kippur, and Other Atonement Days

Chelsea House
An imprint of Infobase Publishing
132 West 31st Street
New York, NY 10001

Library of Congress Cataloging-in-Publication Data

Hackney Blackwell, Amy
  Lent, Yom Kippur, and other Atonement days/Amy Hackney Blackwell.
     p.cm.— (Holidays and celebrations)
  Includes bibligraphical references and index.
   ISBN 978-1-60413-100-0 (alk.paper)
1. Lent—Juvenile literature. 2. Yom Kippur—Juvenile literature. 3. Fasts and feasts—Juvenile literature. 4. Atonement—Juvenile literature. I. Title. II. Series.
 BV85.H24 2009
  202'.2—dc22
                              2009010109

Produced by Print Matters, Inc.
Text design by A Good Thing, Inc.
Cover design by Alicia Post
Cover printed by Creative Printing
Book printed and bound by Creative Printing
Date printed: June, 2010
Printed in China

10 9 8 7 6 5 4 3 2

Contents

࿔

Introduction to Holidays and Celebrations

Holidays mark time. They occupy a space outside of ordinary events and give shape and meaning to our everyday existence. They also remind us of the passage of time as we reflect on Christmases, Passovers, or Ramadans past. Throughout human history, nations and peoples have marked their calendars with special days to celebrate, commemorate, and memorialize. We set aside times to reflect on the past and future, to rest and renew physically and spiritually, and to simply have fun.

In English we call these extraordinary moments "holidays," a contraction of the term "holy day." Sometimes holidays are truly holy days—the Sabbath, Easter, or Eid al-Fitr, for example—but they can also be nonreligious occasions that serve political purposes, address the social needs of communities and individuals, or focus on regional customs and games.

This series explores the meanings and celebrations of holidays across religions and cultures around the world. It groups the holidays into volumes according to theme (such as *Lent, Yom Kippur, and Other Atonement Days; Thanksgiving and Other Harvest Festivals; Independence Days; Easter, Passover, and Other Spring Festivals; Western and Chinese New Year's Celebrations; Religious New Year's Celebrations; Carnival; Ramadan,* and *Halloween and Commemorations of the Dead*) or by their common human experience due to their closeness on the calendar (such as *Christmas and Hanukkah*). Each volume is divided into two sections—the first introduces readers to the origins, history, and common practices associated with the holidays; and the second section takes the reader on a worldwide tour that shows the regional variations and distinctive celebrations within specific countries. The reader will learn how these holidays started, what they mean to the people who celebrate them, and how different cultures celebrate them. These volumes have an international focus, and thus readers will be able to learn about diversity both at home and throughout the world.

We can learn a great deal about a people or nation by the holidays they celebrate. We can also learn from holidays how cultures and religions have interacted and mingled over time. We see in celebrations not just the past through tradition, but the principles and traits that people embrace and value today.

The Chelsea House Holidays and Celebrations series surveys this rich and varied festive terrain. Its 10 volumes show the distinct ways that people all over the world infuse ordinary life with meaning, purpose, or joy. The series cannot be all-inclusive or the last word on so vast a subject, but it offers a vital first step for those eager to learn more about the diverse, fascinating, and vibrant cultures of the world, through the festivity that gives expression, order, and meaning to their lives.

Residents smile as a Filipino Catholic priest sprinkles holy water on palm fronds outside a church in the Philippines. The religious tradition is observed every Lent in this predominantly Roman Catholic country to commemorate the triumphant entry of Jesus into Jerusalem.

Introduction

Regardless of who we are, we all make mistakes. Sometimes these mistakes can gather in our minds and make it difficult for us to progress in our lives. We yearn for a chance to start over, to right our wrongs, and to create a better future by improving upon our pasts. Though it is impossible to be perfect, we can significantly improve ourselves through a combination of will, effort, and humility.

Several religious holidays around the world are devoted to this very task. These holidays are called *days of atonement*. Atonement is the act of acknowledging one's sins and asking them to be forgiven. On days of atonement, people are given a chance to earn God's forgiveness. This is done through a process of repentance, or the act of expressing sorrow for one's sins, and penance, a form of suffering one puts upon him- or herself to make up for previous misdeeds.

Ultra-Orthodox Jews pray during morning prayers at the Western Wall, Judaism's holiest site in Jerusalem. Leading into the Jewish holiday of Yom Kippur, observant Jews say special prayers early in the morning, asking forgiveness for the sins committed in the past year.

Three major atonement observances are Lent, Yom Kippur, and Vassa (primarily known as Rains Retreat). Muslims in southern Asia, particularly those in India and Pakistan, observe Shab-i Barat, a day of atonement that shares with Yom Kippur the idea that as the faithful pray, Allah (God) determines their destinies for the coming year. Ramadan, observed by Muslims everywhere, focuses on renewal and rededication to spiritual purpose. (For details on this holiday see the volume called *Ramadan*.) Other days of atonement not discussed in this volume but integral to select nations and regions include the Dipri festival held by the Abijdji tribe in the Ivory Coast; the Igbi festival held in the Dagestan region in Russia; the Loi Krathong Festival held in Thailand; and the Thaipusam (Thai Poosam) festival celebrated in India, Malaysia, Sri Lanka, Singapore, South Africa, and elsewhere. These observances are a sampling of the diverse ways that people aspire to be better. In this volume the discussion focuses on the atonement holidays of principal importance to communities world-wide and across time.

Lent is a Christian holiday, Yom Kippur is a Jewish holiday, and Rains Retreat is a Buddhist holiday. Not all Christians observe Lent, but many do. For most Roman Catholics, Eastern Orthodox, and some Protestant Christians, Lent is one of the most spiritually important times of the year. Similarly, Yom Kippur is one of the most important holidays of the Jewish calendar. Even Jews who rarely participate in religious rituals go to synagogue and pray during Yom Kippur. Rains Retreat is central to the life of the followers of Theravada Buddhism. The other main branch of Buddhism, Mahayana Buddhism, has abandoned the holiday.

Although these atonement days differ in their customs, traditions, locations, and beliefs, all have one thing in common: the desire of their observers to lead fuller, more enriched lives that better contribute to the local and global community. Each of these observances provides such an opportunity for those willing to undertake it.

Lent

Lent refers to the 40 days that precede the Christian holiday of Easter. The 40 days symbolize the amount of time Jesus is believed to have retreated to the desert to prepare for his crucifixion and face the temptations of Satan. He overcame these temptations by reciting scripture, praying, and fasting. (Fasting is when someone goes without food, goes without certain foods, or eats very little.) Today, Christians practice these things in addition to giving alms, or gifts, to those in need during Lent. It is a time of sacrifice and reflection that aims to imitate the struggles and triumphs of Jesus' time in the desert. It is also a time to consider the sacrifice he made when dying on the cross to redeem humanity from sin. Christians attempt to make personal sacrifices in a gesture of gratitude and humility. Lent concludes on Easter Sunday, when Christians celebrate Jesus' resurrection and victory over sin.

A woman leaves a church with a cross of ash on her forehead after attending Mass in observance of Ash Wednesday in La Paz, Bolivia. Ash Wednesday begins the austere period of personal sacrifice and reflection known as Lent.

Origins of Lent

Christianity

Christians believe that Jesus, also known as Christ, or Jesus Christ, was the son of God who was born on Earth to teach people about God. He spent several years preaching to the Jews of Israel and then was arrested and executed by the Romans. The Romans executed him by nailing him to a cross and leaving him to hang there until he died (an accepted form of execution for the Romans of that time). Jesus' death is considered the sacrifice that God, and Jesus, made to make it possible for believers to have their sins forgiven so that they can go to Heaven after they die. Today the cross is a symbol of Christianity throughout the world.

There are many denominations, or types, of Christianity throughout the world. There are differences in the way Christianity is practiced between the Western and Eastern Churches and between the Roman Catholic and Protestant faiths. Because of these distinctions, there are many ways of observing Lent.

By the 11th century, Christianity had spread in its various forms throughout most of the Western world as well as some way into the Far East. In 1054, however, a group of Christians based in what is present-day Turkey rejected the authority of the Roman Catholic Church over Eastern patriarchs. The pope forced this group to leave the Church. They kept hold of their beliefs and became known as the Eastern Orthodox Church. The Catholic Church began to identify itself as the "Western" Church because for most of the medieval period (from approximately 500 to 1500) the center of its leadership was in Rome, one of the largest cities in western Europe. It was also known simply as the Roman Catholic Church, a name it retains to this day.

In 1517 there was another division within the Roman Catholic Church. A group of reformers led by the German theologian Martin

Where Jesus Was Crucified

Calvary and *Golgotha* are the English-language Western Christian names given to the site, outside of ancient Jerusalem's early first-century walls, ascribed to Jesus' crucifixion.

Luther advocated drastic changes within the structure of the Church. Among these was the rejection of the way the pope and certain priests could become wealthy and powerful. They saw this as going directly against the teachings of Jesus. Those who agreed with Martin Luther and his fellow reformers separated from the Roman Catholic Church and began the Protestant Church.

Members of each of these Churches currently live all over the world. Eastern Orthodoxy is the second-largest Christian denomination after Roman Catholicism, and includes the Greek and Russian Orthodox Churches. The Western Churches include the original Roman Catholic Church and various Protestant denominations such as the Anglican Communion, and the Methodist and Presbyterian Churches.

The Council of Nicea and the First Mention of Lent

The word *Lent* is an Anglo-Saxon word meaning "spring." Anglo-Saxon, also known as Old English, is a Germanic language that was spoken in the British Isles from the fifth through the 11th centuries. It gradually evolved into modern English between the 11th and 17th centuries.

The practice of Lent is much older than the English word for the season. In the early days of Christianity, Lent was called *tessarakoste*, "fortieth" in Greek, or *quadragesima*, "fortieth day" in Latin. The first mention of the word *tessarakoste* appears in documents from a meeting church leaders held in the year 325 called the Council of Nicea (at which the Nicene Creed, or statement of beliefs, was developed). It is based on the Greek word *pentekoste*, or "fiftieth," which was the word for the Jewish festival known as Pentecost, the celebration of the 50th day after Passover (the holiday celebrating the exodus of the Israelites from Egyptian slavery).

Historians do not know exactly when Christians began observing Lent. Early medieval church scholars believed that Jesus' apostles introduced the tradition of 40 days of fasting, but there is no historical evidence to support this. (Jesus' apostles were the 12 men he chose to preach his teachings both during and after his life.) It appears that Christians during the first three centuries of the Common Era gradually worked out the details of the religious observance. Christian scholars note that some Christians fasted in the period before Easter, but it does not appear that there was any tradition of a 40-day fast. Rather, it seems to have begun as a one- or two-day fast just before Easter. Historians Irenaeus (ca. 130 200) and Tertullian (ca. 160 or 170–ca. 230) note this type of fast in writings from the late second and early third centuries.

In the year 331, the early Christian bishop Athanasius of Alexandria, Egypt, recommended that believers fast for 40 days before Holy Week, the last week before Easter. By the fifth century, the observance of Lent was a common practice in the Roman Catholic world. In Rome Lent lasted six weeks, although people may not have fasted for the entire period. In Jerusalem, some Christians observed Lent for eight weeks, which resulted in 40 total days of fasting (Saturday and Sunday were not fast days). By this time, Holy Week had become institutionalized throughout the different regions. Holy Week was characterized by particularly severe fasting, such as the "black fast" on Holy Saturday, the day on which Jesus is said to have lain in his tomb. This type of fast allows the believer only one meal to be taken after sunset and is usually limited to bread and water alone.

When Lent Is Observed

The Western and Eastern Churches both observe Lent, but at different times and with different rituals. Various cultures also celebrate differently; for example, Catholics in the United States have different Lenten customs from Catholics in Brazil or Zimbabwe. The dates of Lent depend on the date of Easter. Easter is called a "movable feast," because it is celebrated on different dates every year. The Western and Eastern Churches celebrate Easter at different times because they use different methods to schedule the holiday.

Roman Catholic and Protestant Churches schedule Easter using a complicated system of rules that date to the Council of Nicea. At that

Worshippers attend the traditional Orthodox Easter service in Russia. Easter marks the end of the 40 days of Lent.

meeting in 325, church leaders came up with a number of rules about how the Roman Catholic Church should work. One thing they decided was that the Church should hold a holiday to commemorate the day on which Jesus rose from the dead. Because they did not know when this happened, they decided that Easter would be celebrated on the Sunday after the first full Moon following the spring equinox. (The spring equinox is the day in March when daylight and darkness are of equal lengths in the Northern Hemisphere.) Helpful astronomers created a chart that plotted out their estimates of the dates of full Moons for many years to come. The Church formally adopted these dates as what are called "Ecclesiastical Full Moons." They noted that the spring equinox fell on March 20 in 325, so they made that an official date. From then on, the rule for scheduling Easter was that Easter should fall on the first Sunday after the first Ecclesiastical Full Moon after March 20. The result of this complicated scheduling is that the Western Easter can fall anywhere between March 22 and April 25.

The Cycle of Easter

The cycle of Easter dates repeats itself every 84 years in the Western Churches. The Easter dates of the Eastern Churches repeat on a 19-year cycle. In other words, Easter this year will fall on the same date as it did 19 years ago and will fall 19 years from now.

The Eastern Orthodox Easter usually comes after the Western Easter. There are several reasons for this. First, the Eastern Churches do not use the same calendar as the Western Churches. Western Churches use the Gregorian calendar, which is the calendar that is used in Canada, Europe, the United States, and most of the world. The Eastern Churches use the Julian calendar, which was the calendar in place when the rules for scheduling Easter were first set. The Julian calendar is currently 13 days ahead of the Gregorian calendar. Second, Eastern Churches use the actual first full Moon after the spring equinox to set the date of Easter. They do not use the Ecclesiastical Full Moons. Third, the Orthodox Easter must fall after the Jewish holiday of Passover. This is to remain faithful to the Bible's claim that Jesus died after Passover. With these regulations, April 3 is the earliest date on which the Eastern Churches can celebrate Easter. Sometimes the Eastern Orthodox Easter falls on the same date as it does for Western Churches. In other years it might be as many as five weeks later.

With the date of Easter in place, the starting date for Lent can be determined. In the Western Church it begins 46 days prior to Easter. Although it is said to last for 40 days, Sundays are not included in the count because they are not considered "fast days." In the Eastern Churches, neither Saturdays nor Sundays are considered fast days, so they do not count toward the 40-day total. To make it 40 days, the Eastern Churches observe seven weeks of Lent (equaling 35 fast days) and an additional week before

Why Is Lent 40 Days?

Scholars suggest several explanations for the length of Lent. The number 40 has a great deal of biblical significance. A few examples of events that could have influenced the early Church's decision to make Lent 40 days are:

- Jesus is believed to have spent 40 days in the desert being tempted by Satan.
- Jesus is said to have lain 40 hours in his tomb after his death.
- Moses spent 40 days on Mount Sinai talking with God.
- Noah and his family and animals survived living on the Ark through 40 days of rain.

Lent called Cheese Week. During this week, believers do not eat meat, so the days count as fast days, but they do eat dairy products and eggs. This is their last opportunity to consume these foods until Easter.

Observing Lent

Getting Ready for Lent: Carnival and Mardi Gras/Shrove Tuesday

Because it is difficult to spend several weeks fasting and repenting, people around the world spend the days before Lent enjoying themselves and eating the food that they will not be able to eat during the Lenten fast. In many places, Christians participate in a celebration called *Carnival*. Carnival can last for several weeks. It is a festive time of parties, parades with elaborate floats and colorful costumes, and large amounts of food and drink.

The day before Lent is the last chance for recreation, silliness, and indulgence in things such as rich foods before the solemn holiday. It is also the day when people are supposed to confess their sins and cleanse their souls in preparation for Lent. These two purposes give the day two of its most common names: Mardi Gras and Shrove Tuesday.

Mardi Gras is French for "Fat Tuesday," another common name for the day before Lent. (*Mardi* is the French word for "Tuesday." *Gras* is the French word for "fat," as in edible fat, such as butter or grease.) Mardi Gras is the day people traditionally eat all the buttery, greasy foods that are not supposed to be eaten during Lent. In many places people will cook a lot of pancakes or crêpes on the day before Lent. This is a way of using up their eggs, milk, and butter before these foods become off-limits. They call this day "Pancake Day."

Mardi Gras

The days leading up to Lent are a time of great festivities in many places. Christians traditionally tried to eat up all their fat and meat before Lent began, which led to large-scale parties. Because for Western Churches Lent always begins on a Wednesday, the Tuesday before that day became the day of the most extreme feasting.

Hard-Boiled Eggs

One reason boiled eggs are associated with Easter is that people could not eat them during Lent, so people would boil them to preserve them. By the time Easter arrived, everyone had a pile of eggs waiting to be eaten.

Shrove Tuesday is "Confession Tuesday." *Shrove* comes from "shrive," an old word that means to have one's sins forgiven through a church ritual called "confession." In this ritual, a person tells his or her sins to a priest. The priest asks God to grant forgiveness to the person confessing and then gives the person different prayers to say as a penance. People traditionally go to confession on Shrove Tuesday so they can begin the Lenten season feeling renewed. Since the next 40 days will be devoted to living in imitation of Jesus, it is important that the previous year's sins be absolved, or taken away, through the act of confession.

Beginning Lent: Monday or Wednesday

In the Roman Catholic and some Protestant Churches, Lent begins on the Wednesday 46 days before Easter. This day is called Ash Wednesday. According to many Christian traditions, Ash Wednesday is a day of repentance. Many Roman Catholics and Episcopalians fast on this day, either refraining from eating meat or eating much less food than usual. In addition, many Catholics and Episcopalians attend

A member of the Flaming Arrows tribe of Mardi Gras Indians shows off his costume during Mardi Gras in New Orleans. Mardi Gras, or Fat Tuesday, represents the end of Carnival season and the beginning of Lent.

Lent Begins

The day after Mardi Gras, everything changes. For Western Churches, Ash Wednesday is the official beginning of Lent each year (the first day of Lent is always on a Wednesday). It is time for people to stop thinking about having a good time and start trying to improve their souls.

a special service where the priest smudges ashes on the foreheads of members of the congregation in the shape of a cross, signifying that they belong to Christ. Believers wear these ashes on their foreheads for the rest of the day. Since ancient times, ashes have been symbolic of repentance because they are what remains after a fire. The ashes also serve as a reminder that all living beings will become dust in the end. In the past, some people covered their entire bodies in ashes on Ash Wednesday as a sign of penance.

In Eastern Christianity, Lent is known as Great Lent or Great Fast. The Eastern Orthodox Church begins Lent on the Monday seven weeks before Easter. The Eastern faithful call this "Clean Monday," and it is a day of fasting and spiritual preparation but also a festive time. The first week of Lent is called Clean Week. On this day, people go out to play and fly kites in the spring breezes. Many people consider Clean Monday the official start of spring. The day has a festive atmosphere quite different from the somber mood prevalent among Western Christians on Ash Wednesday.

The night before Great Lent begins, believers go to church for a special service dedicated to confession of sins. The readings during this service emphasize the need to do well and encourage believers to purify their souls. After the readings, everyone bows to one another and asks forgiveness for anything they have done wrong during the past year. This is a way of beginning the Great Lent with a clean conscience— not only with God, but with neighbors, as well.

Clean Week

In the Orthodox Church, Great Lent begins on Clean Monday. Clean Monday is a festive public holiday in Greece and Cyprus.

A Catholic woman, with a cross of ashes on her forehead, prays during the observance of Ash Wednesday in San Jose, Costa Rica.

The First Weeks of Lent

Christian churches go through a standard cycle of weeks during Lent. Each week is associated with a particular religious event or reading from the biblical accounts of the life of Jesus called the Gospels.

For the weeks of Lent, from Ash Wednesday to Palm Sunday (the Sunday before Easter), each Sunday's church service is devoted to a particular lesson, such as overcoming temptation or recovering from having done something wrong. As Christians of both the Eastern and Western Churches progress through their Lenten journey, it is important that they have examples to follow in order to become better, more saintly people. By attending these services each week and hearing stories of the good deeds of Jesus and his followers, they are given inspiration for their own difficult passage through Lent. Western and Eastern Churches emphasize different themes on each day but share the belief that learning to live in imitation of the Gospels becomes much less overwhelming when broken down to one lesson at a time.

The Western Church has a cycle of Lenten Sundays, each of which has a particular set of gospel readings associated with it:

First Sunday: The Temptation of Christ
Second Sunday: The Transfiguration
Third Sunday: The story of the Samaritan woman
Fourth Sunday: The story of the man born
                blind, or the Prodigal Son

Fifth Sunday:	The woman charged with adultery and the raising of Lazarus
Sixth Sunday:	Palm Sunday
Seventh Sunday: (conclusion)	Easter Sunday

In the Eastern Orthodox Church, the Great Lent Sundays are paired with these themes:

First Sunday:	Sunday of Orthodoxy
Second Sunday:	St. Gregory Palamas
Third Sunday:	Adoration of the Cross
Fourth Sunday:	St. John of Climax
Fifth Sunday:	St. Mary of Egypt
Sixth Sunday:	Palm Sunday
Seventh Sunday: (conclusion)	Easter Sunday

Passiontide: The Last Two Weeks of Lent

Passiontide is the last two weeks of Lent. Observed primarily by traditional Catholics and Anglicans, it begins on a day called Passion Sunday, one week before Palm Sunday. On Passion Sunday, some Catholics engage in a prayer called the "Forty Hours' Devotion," which consists of 40 hours of continuous prayer said in a series of different churches by different people—sort of like a prayer relay, with people taking turns praying. Other traditions include covering the altar and veiling the statues and crucifixes in purple cloth. Traditionally, purple is regarded as a royal color and a purple cloth on the altar acts as a reminder that Jesus is king. The cloth is removed on Easter Sunday to symbolize the resurrection of Christ. Passiontide also has its own kind of music. Solemn and mournful, it has been written throughout the years by composers inspired by the suffering and death of Jesus.

Lenten Decorations

Catholic churches change their decorations from purple to red on Palm Sunday. Red symbolizes blood, martyrs, and the death of Christ. Most Protestant churches decorate in purple for the entire Lenten season.

The Last Week of Lent: Holy Week/ Great and Holy Week

The last week of Lent is called *Holy Week* in the Western Churches, and *Great and Holy Week* in the Eastern. During this week, believers remember

The Days of Holy Week and Great and Holy Week

Holy Week and Great and Holy Week include some of the most important days of the Christian calendar:

- Palm Sunday, the Sunday before Easter, is the day on which Jesus is said to have entered the city of Jerusalem for the Jewish holiday Passover. The people of Jerusalem laid palm branches on the ground in front of him.

- Holy Monday is said to be the day on which Jesus cursed a fig tree and turned the merchants out of the Temple of Jerusalem.

- Holy Tuesday is the day on which Jesus is said to have preached in the Temple.

- Holy Wednesday is sometimes called Spy Wednesday because this is the day on which the apostle Judas Iscariot is said to have conspired with the Jewish priests to have Jesus arrested.

- Holy Thursday, or Maundy Thursday, commemorates the day on which Jesus and his apostles shared the Last Supper, after which they went to the Garden of Gethsemane. Later that evening Jesus was betrayed by Judas and tried for crucifixion.

- Good Friday commemorates the day on which Jesus was crucified and died.

- Holy Saturday is the day on which Jesus is said to have lain in his tomb.

- Holy Week or Great and Holy Week ends with Easter Sunday, the day on which Jesus is believed to have risen from the dead.

the events in the last week of Jesus' life. These include Jesus' entrance into Jerusalem and his suffering on the way to crucifixion, which are sometimes called the "Passion of Jesus Christ," or "Passion of Christ."

During Holy Week, Christians begin to look ahead to Jesus' resurrection and the celebration of Easter. Believers observe the week in various ways. Some Christians attend more religious services than usual. They may participate in the Stations of the Cross, a ritual where believers go through the events leading up to Jesus' crucifixion, or attend passion plays, reenactments of the stations themselves. Members of the Greek Orthodox faith of the Eastern Church make it a practice to clean their houses as well as their souls. They remove clutter from closets and cupboards and repaint walls on the inside and outside of their homes. In regions with a Spanish colonial heritage, Holy Week can be a weeklong celebration that is both somber and festive. It may include outdoor gatherings for prayer and slow, quiet processions through the streets.

Palm Sunday

Holy Week begins with Palm Sunday, the Sunday before Easter. This is the day on which Jesus is said to have entered the city of Jerusalem to celebrate Passover. The people of the city laid palm branches before him. At church services on Palm Sunday, many churches hand out palm fronds, or branches, to attendees, symbolizing the palm fronds that the people

The Arrival of Jesus in Jerusalem

In the book of Matthew, one of the four Gospels, Jesus is described as riding into Jerusalem on a donkey. In some Eastern traditions, the donkey was seen as an animal of peace, whereas the horse was an animal of war. The fact that Jesus rides a donkey carries a message of peace and humility. However, the book of John admits that the crowd might not have interpreted the symbolism correctly. It states, "These things understood not His disciples at the first" (John 12:16). It is possible that the public saw Jesus' triumphant entry into Jerusalem as a declaration of war against Israel's enemies rather than as an expression of peaceful intentions.

of Jerusalem laid before Jesus as he entered the city. Even during pre-Christian times, it was traditional to show respect to honored personages by covering their path in some way as they entered a city or building. Just as today a red carpet is rolled out for celebrities or political figures, in ancient times people would lay down flowers, plant fronds, or even their garments for a person to walk or ride over.

While some churches give pieces of palm to the people who attend services, in other areas, people buy their own palm fronds and bring them to church to be blessed. Often church members weave their palm fronds into crosses and other shapes that have religious meanings. Although some of the palms were traditionally burned to make ashes for the following year's Ash Wednesday, believers today often save them to display in their houses.

In areas where it is difficult to obtain palm fronds, other branches such as pussy willows, yew, or spruce are substituted. Greek Orthodox churches give their parishioners bay leaves instead of palm fronds. Bay is a type of laurel tree. In ancient Greek and Roman times it had special

A young woman sells palms outside the Cathedral in Tegucigalpa, Honduras, the day before Palm Sunday.

significance, as poets and victorious soldiers would be honored with crowns woven of its branches. It is also good for cooking. In some homes leaves that have been blessed in church are taken home and used for this purpose during Holy Week.

Holy or Maundy Thursday

The Thursday before Easter, often called Maundy Thursday, is an important day in many churches. It is the day on which Jesus and his apostles are said to have eaten the Last Supper prior to his arrest in the Garden of Gethsemane. Anglican and other Protestant churches often hold special Communion services to commemorate the Last Supper. This is the final meal Jesus shared with his apostles. Jesus is said to have washed the feet of the apostles before the beginning of the Last Supper. In those days, everyone wore sandals and their feet got dirty. When people invited guests into their houses, the hosts would bring out water for the guests to wash their feet when they arrived. Often, the hosts would perform the foot washing themselves. This was an act of humility and of hospitality to make the guests feel welcome. By washing his apostles' feet, Jesus was showing humility and acting like a good host.

Many churches hold ceremonies on Holy Thursday in which a priest washes the feet of 12 parishioners as a sign of humility. The Bible reading will often be from the Gospel of John, which recounts Jesus' act of foot washing. In many North American churches 12 parishioners will play the roles of Jesus' 12 apostles. The priest or minister will move from person to person and wash each of their feet. This allows the person doing the washing to demonstrate humility and charity, while putting the recipients in the unusual position of accepting an intimate service from a person of authority. Washing of the feet is also a way of linking baptism with the

The Meaning of *Maundy*

The name "Maundy Thursday" comes from a line in the Latin version of the Gospel of John, "Mandatum novum do vobis ut diligatis invicem sicut dilexi vos," which means, "A new commandment I give to you, that you love one another as I have loved you." The word *mandatum*, meaning "command," gradually turned into the English "Maundy."

A girl touches a crucifix during an Orthodox Good Friday service in Macedonia. The Orthodox Church observes Easter according to the Julian calendar.

communal meal of the Last Supper. Both practices use water as a symbol of cleansing and rebirth.

Good Friday

Good Friday is said to be the day of Jesus' crucifixion and death. This is a sad day for many Christians, because Jesus spent the day in pain, being whipped and nailed to the cross, and then dying. Fasting is a way of remembering the events of the day. Many Christians fast or avoid eating meat on Good Friday even if they never observe fast days during the rest of the year. Jesus is said to have hung on the cross for three hours before he died. Some churches observe this event by holding a three-hour mourning service during the afternoon to mark Jesus' suffering.

Holy Saturday

Holy Saturday is the day before Easter. This is the day Jesus is said to have lain in the tomb after his death. There are no special services during this day, though Catholic and Greek Orthodox churches often baptize new members, both infants and converts, on Holy Saturday because the day is especially holy, marking the day before Jesus' victory over death. Often, churches hold evening vigil services to anticipate Jesus' resurrection on Easter morning. In many religious communities, Holy Saturday is a day of rigorous fasting, intense prayer, and even the removal of items such as statues and icons from the church. This is done to focus the mind, body, and soul completely on the burial of Jesus, and to raise anticipation for his resurrection the following day.

Fasting

Throughout the history of Lent there have been a wide variety of fasting practices. In the fifth century B.C.E., the Greek historian Socrates observed that some people ate nothing, some ate only dry bread, some avoided nuts and eggs, some abstained from the flesh of all living creatures, some avoided meat but ate fish and poultry, and some ate nothing during the day but ate whatever they wanted during the evening. Early Christian leaders envisioned stricter fasting rules in which Christians would go without food for 24 hours at a time periodically throughout Lent, and eat no more than one or two meals during Holy Week. In practice, the Catholic Church's general rule for fast days was to eat no more than one meal on a fast day, and this meal could be eaten only in the evening. Meat and wine were forbidden in the early days of the Church, though wine soon became an acceptable part of fast day meals.

During the medieval period in Europe, it became common for people to avoid particular foods during Lent. Eggs, butter, cheese, and milk were the most typical. Many people gave up eating meat as well. The reason for this was that dairy products, eggs, and meat were considered rich, indulgent foods that were pleasant to eat. For example, bread with butter is tastier and more satisfying than plain bread. The idea behind fasting was to give up indulgences, so people deliberately avoided rich foods. Fish was traditionally not considered meat, so it became common to eat fish on fast days. The medieval church would sometimes let people break religious rules in exchange for donations of money. In Germany and France, many people gave money to the church in order to be able to eat butter during Lent.

As time went on, there were official rules set by the Roman Catholic Church for fast days and days of abstinence. On fast days, people between the ages of 18 and 59 were limited to one full meal or two small meals. On abstinence days, everyone over the age of 14 was supposed to avoid eating meat or poultry. Over the years the Church has relaxed its rules on fasting, allowing meat on many days during Lent. Many Christians today do not fast at all, or limit their fasting to avoiding meat on Good Friday; instead they might give up activities or specific foods they particularly enjoy.

Eastern Orthodox believers have their own rules for fasting. People who observe the fast do not eat meat from animals with backbones (mammals, birds, and fish) or products from animals with red blood (milk, eggs, and other dairy products). They also avoid olive oil and wine. All of these are considered rich foods, and giving them up is a real sacrifice

Russian children eating during Great Lent. Eastern Orthodox believers avoid meat, dairy products, olive oil, and wine during Lent.

for many people. This helps them feel that they are making up for their sins.

Sacrifices

Many Christians try to make sacrifices during Lent. Today it is very common for people to give up activities they enjoy, not just foods that they consider indulgent or bad for them. Some people may stop eating chocolate or drinking alcohol, whereas others might give up their nightly habit of watching television or playing computer games. People also try to do good deeds, such as volunteering at a soup kitchen or collecting clothing for the poor. These sacrifices are meant to be similar to the sacrifice Jesus made for believers when he died on the cross for their sins, though much less extreme. They encourage people to think of others before themselves, and serve as reminders of the values that Jesus expressed in his teachings, such as kindness and tolerance toward others. These sacrifices are not formal and churches do not enforce them. Often a believer will not even tell anyone that he or she has given up something for Lent. The sacrifice is a personal matter, and only the person who makes it will know if he or she succeeds or fails at keeping the resolution all the way through Lent.

Stations of the Cross

The Stations of the Cross, also called the Way of the Cross, Via Crucis, Via Dolorosa, or the Way of Sorrows, is a ritual where believers go through the events leading up to Jesus' crucifixion. Many Catholic and some Protestant churches have 14 pictures or statues arranged around the church, each depicting one of the 14 stations. Believers participating in the ritual can walk from image to image and contemplate the events.

At each station, people participating in the ritual consider the image, meditate on its meaning, and say a prayer. Many people participate in Stations of the Cross ceremonies on Good Friday and the other Fridays during Lent, though the ritual can be done at any time.

In some places, groups of believers reenact the stations themselves in processions through the streets. Actors and non-actors alike play the parts of Jesus, the apostles, the Roman guards, Pontius Pilate, Herod, and other figures central to the event of the crucifixion. This is known as a "passion play." Passion plays are very popular during Holy Week. They can be performed anywhere, from a church to a street to a stage. Sometimes reenactments get a little more physical, as in the Philippines, where participants in the Moriones Festival actually shed their own blood in their public displays of devotion and acts of penance. Other reenactments may have a different emphasis as in Syria, where the Lent of Jonah is performed, inspired by the biblical story of Jonah, who was delivered by whale to the city of Nineveh in time to warn the citizens to repent before God exercised his wrath against them.

Yom Kippur

Yom Kippur is the Jewish Day of Atonement. It is the most sacred day of the Jewish year. According to Jewish tradition, on Yom Kippur God closes the Book of Life for the past year and determines how the upcoming year will go for each believer. Those who repent for their sins will have a good year; those who do not may have a bad one.

Origins of Yom Kippur
Judaism

Of the three Abrahamic religions—religions that consider Abraham to be a founder and central prophet (Judaism, Christianity, and Islam)—Judaism is the oldest. Judaism is a monotheistic religion; it supports a single, all-knowing God who created the universe and functions as its ongoing overseer. In ancient times, Jews worshiped in two great Temples in Jerusalem, each of which was destroyed. Central to Judaism is the concept of the covenant, or agreement, between God and his people that began with Abraham, in which God has chosen Jews to be a light to the nations, and they have accepted the greater responsibilities and obligations that God's law requires. Moses, too, is central to Judaism. According to Jewish tradition, God's Ten Commandments, or rules for human conduct, were given to Moses and the Israelites on Mount Sinai.

Indian Jewish women pray at the *hekhal*, an ornamental closet that contains a synagogue's Torah scrolls, after a prayer ceremony marking Yom Kippur in Mumbai, India. Judaism was one of the earliest religions to arrive in India.

The Ten Commandments

The Ten Commandments are:

1. I am the Lord your God, and you shall have no other gods besides me.
2. You shall not make for yourself a sculptured image and shall not bow down to or serve idols
3. You shall not take in vain the name of the Lord.
4. Remember the Sabbath day and keep it holy.
5. Honor your father and your mother.
6. You shall not murder.
7. You shall not commit adultery.
8. You shall not steal.
9. You shall not bear false witness against your neighbor.
10. You shall not covet your neighbor's wife or possessions.

Although Catholics and Protestants use the same ancient text, they have a slightly different set of commandments.

Today there are two main cultural groups of Jews: the Ashkenazi Jews and the Sephardic Jews. *Ashkenazi* is an old Hebrew word for "Germany" and originally indicated Jews who spoke Yiddish, a German dialect. Many of them were driven from their homes and forced to emigrate during the 19th and 20th centuries by anti-Semitic attacks. "Ashkenazi" has come to include Jews from northern and eastern Europe and their descendants in the Americas. *Sephardic* is derived from the old Hebrew word for "Spain." The Sephardic Jews are descended from Jews who lived in Spain during the medieval period. The Spanish rulers forced them to leave Spain during the 1400s. Today "Sephardic" includes the eastern Jews of Mediterranean, Balkan, Aegean, and Middle Eastern lands and their descendants living in the Americas.

In religious observance, Jews array in three main categories: Reform, Conservative, and Orthodox. These groups differ in their interpretations of the will of God, especially as it relates to their adherence to the religious laws and codes for living set out in the Holy Scriptures (principally the book of Leviticus). Orthodox Jews believe that the Torah, their religious text (and an important part of the Christian Bible and Muslim Quran as well), is the word of God and a guide for all behavior. The Reform and Conservative Jews place equal weight on the Torah but interpret it less literally than Orthodox Jews. Reform and Conservative Jews may hold religious services in languages other than Hebrew and tend to follow the ancient biblical codes less strictly than do Orthodox Jews.

Moses and the First Yom Kippur

Yom Kippur is a very ancient festival. The book of Leviticus in the Hebrew scriptures (the latter known as the Old Testament to Christians; it includes the Torah, or Five Books of Moses) describes many of the rituals practiced today. According to tradition, Yom Kippur is the day when God gave Moses the second set of the Ten Commandments. It is also the day when the Israelites were forgiven for worshipping a Golden Calf that represented God instead of God Himself, a sight that had caused Moses to break the first set of Ten Commandments in anger.

Moses was a Hebrew leader who was born and raised in Egypt. During his life, the Hebrew people were living in Egypt, enslaved by the Egyptians. Moses led the Hebrew slaves out of Egypt and across the Red Sea, promising that he would take them to the homeland God had promised them in Israel. The Hebrews, or Israelites, wandered in the desert for 40 years on their way to this promised land. While they were wandering, God called Moses up to the top of Mount Horeb, where God gave him the Ten Commandments, 10 laws that told the Hebrews how to live. When Moses descended from the mountain 40 days later, he discovered that the Israelites had grown frightened in his absence and decided to give up on worshipping God. They were instead worshipping a statue in the shape of a Golden Calf that Aaron, Moses' older brother, had agreed to build. God was angry with the Israelites and wanted to destroy them, but Moses persuaded him not to. He then persuaded the Israelites to give up the Golden Calf and worship God instead. The story of Moses is in the book of Exodus.

By the beginning of the Common Era, Jewish religious leaders had developed a complex series of rituals associated with Yom Kippur. These involved ritual baths in a special kind of religious bath called a *mikvah*, several changes of clothing, fasting, and a series of prayers and sacrifices. Through these acts, the religious leaders cleansed the Jewish people of the previous year's sins and prepared them for the following year.

When Yom Kippur Is Observed

Yom Kippur takes place on the 10th day of the seventh month in the Hebrew calendar, Tishri. It always follows Rosh Hashanah, the Jewish New Year, which occurs on the first day of Tishri. These two holidays and the period of time between them are known as the High Holy Days in Jewish tradition.

Yom Kippur falls on a different day every year in the Gregorian calendar (which marks months based on the cycles of the Sun) because the Hebrew calendar marks months based on the cycles of the Moon. Twelve lunar cycles add up to about 354 days, 11 days shorter than the time it takes Earth to travel around the Sun. To make up for this difference, an extra month is inserted into the Hebrew calendar every few years. That way, the months and seasons continue to correspond with one another. Rosh Hashanah and Yom Kippur always fall in the early autumn, in September or October of the Western calendar. Another difference between the Gregorian and the Jewish calendars is that in the Jewish calendar a day begins at sundown, while days start at 12 A.M. in the Gregorian calendar.

Observing Yom Kippur

Yom Kippur is a total Sabbath (day of rest), when work of any kind is prohibited. Jews observe Yom Kippur in several ways. The five customs considered the most important are: abstinence from food and drink for 25 hours, beginning a half hour before sunset on the day before Yom Kippur and ending after sundown the next day; no bathing of any kind; no use of perfumes or lotions; no wearing of leather shoes; and no sexual activity. Giving up these indulgences helps people focus on religious thoughts and atoning for their sins. Additionally, Jews often wear white on Yom Kippur as a symbol of purity. Some Jewish men own a garment called a *kittel*, which is a white robe similar to a burial shroud that they can wear over their ordinary clothing.

Elul: The Month before Yom Kippur

Some Conservative and Orthodox Jews in North America observe the month of Elul, the sixth month of the Hebrew calendar, with customs that are similar to those practiced by Christians observing Lent. Elul takes place in August or September of the Georgian calendar and precedes Tishri, the month of the High Holy Days. Many Jewish immigrants who came to the United States in the 20th century used this month to meditate in preparation for Yom Kippur.

It is customary to begin each day of Elul by blowing shofars, or rams' horns, as a way to call one forth to prayer. Shofars are made from real ram's horns (from real male sheep), and so they come in all shapes and sizes. Getting noise out of a shofar is not easy. Some people try to blow it as if it were a trumpet or other brass instrument, placing it against the lower lip and vibrating both lips. Other players recommend placing the mouthpiece inside the mouth and letting the inside of the lower lip provide the vibration. Of course if the mouthpiece is too big, that will not work. Rabbis, or teachers of Jewish laws and custom, counsel that the

A rabbi in Atlanta, Georgia, blows a shofar at Yom Kippur services.

skill of playing is not the point, anyway. What matters is that the shofar-blower have the proper spiritual intention.

Ten Days of Repentance

The Ten Days of Repentance are the 10 days that begin with Rosh Hashanah and end with Yom Kippur. These days are the last chance for Jews to correct wrongs and seek forgiveness for their sins before starting anew after Yom Kippur. Observant Jews may attend several extra services at the synagogue during this period.

A large part of Yom Kippur is asking forgiveness of others. Jews have until sundown on Yom Kippur to seek forgiveness from those they have wronged. Family members and friends are supposed to speak directly to one another and ask forgiveness for sins committed during the previous year. Sometimes people confess specific sins and say that they are sorry. They may instead use ritual words. It is important that the person asking forgiveness looks the other person in the eye and is truly sorry for his or her sins.

Erev Yom Kippur: The Day before Yom Kippur

Erev Yom Kippur is the day before Yom Kippur. On this day, Jews may eat a large meal in preparation for their fast, begin their personal and spiritual reflecting, and take a ritual bath. They may also perform a ritual called *kapparot* or *kapparos*. This ritual is not mentioned in the Torah; it seems to have originated in the seventh century, when most Jews were spread throughout the lands bordering the Mediterranean Sea.

An ultra-Orthodox Jewish man swings a chicken over a child's head while performing the *kapparot* ritual at dawn on the eve of Yom Kippur, the holiest day in the Jewish year, in Jerusalem. Religious Jews believe their sins are transferred from the past year onto the chicken when they pray and wave the chicken over their heads. The fowl is later slaughtered and given to charity.

During *kapparot*, one acquires a live chicken to serve as a receptacle for his or her sins. Every person needs his or her own chicken, and even children participate. Men usually choose roosters and women choose hens. Each person takes the chicken and whirls it over his or her heard three times while reciting a prayer. The chicken is then killed, an act believed to destroy the sins of the believer and create an offering for charity. It is customary to donate the slaughtered chickens to the poor for their feast before Yom Kippur.

Not all Jews practice *kapparot*. Many rabbis disagree with the practice because they think it is a pagan ritual that is not a true part of the Jewish religion. They believe people should pray and meditate instead of conducting ritual sacrifices to get rid of their sins. Today the custom of *kapparot* is not as common as it once was. It is most common among the Haredi Jews, who are especially strict in their beliefs; there are large communities of Haredi Jews in Brooklyn, New York, and Israel. Other Jewish groups sometimes perform the ritual using money tied up in handkerchiefs instead of chickens. The money is then donated to charity. This is a popular option in modern urban and suburban Jewish communities, where the rise of ideas about animal rights have come in conflict with this ancient tradition.

On Erev Yom Kippur most Jews eat a large meal. This meal must tide them over for the next 25 hours so it is usually substantial. Though the ritual of *kapparot* is not as prevalent as it used to be, chicken remains a staple food at these meals. Even for those who do not participate in *kapparot*, charity is important on Erev Yom Kippur. Those who can afford it try to give something to the poor, either directly or through a local charitable organization.

The final tradition of Erev Yom Kippur is a ritual bath called a *mikvah*. A *mikvah* is a public bath with tubs filled with natural "living water," such as a natural spring or well. To bathe at a *mikvah*, Jews must immerse themselves completely. That means they must get into the tub and duck under the water so that their hair is completely soaked.

Jewish Dietary Laws

Many Jews keep "kosher," which means they only eat foods that have been prepared according to Jewish laws and approved by religious leaders. Jews who observe these laws do so throughout the year, not just during holy times.

Natural Water

Mikvahs must be filled by natural water, such as flowing stream water or rainwater. *Mikvahs* are designed so that the water in the bath stays fresh no matter how many people use it.

Orthodox Jews believe they must immerse themselves in a *mikvah* before all Sabbaths and all holidays including Yom Kippur. This is necessary to become clean and renewed before the holiday. The *mikvah* must meet certain conditions to be considered for use. Most important is the bath's connection to a spring or other naturally running water for purity and replenishment.

Yom Kippur

Yom Kippur officially begins at sundown of Erev Yom Kippur. About a half hour before sunset, Jews gather at the synagogue for a special service. At this service many Jewish men wear a prayer shawl called a *tallit* on their heads. (Ordinarily they only wear a *tallit* during morning prayers; the Yom Kippur evening service is the only evening service at which men wear *tallits*.) Fathers bless their sons and daughters at the doorway. Inside the synagogue, people light 25-hour candles to burn during the hours of the holiday as a memorial for dead ancestors. The cantor, a singer trained in leading prayers, chants the Kol Nidre (meaning "All Vows"). Unlike most Jewish prayers, which are in Hebrew, this prayer is in a language called Aramaic. In the prayer, the cantor states that any vows the members of the congregation make over the next year will not be valid. This is to protect

Sacred Hospitality

It is considered polite to invite strangers home to share the family meal after Yom Kippur as a way of extending hospitality throughout the community, both Jewish and non-Jewish.

Rosh Hashanah, the Jewish New Year, and Yom Kippur, the Day of Atonement, are so closely linked in Judaism that together they are known as the High Holy Days. Here, a selection of symbolic foods that have a place in the classic Rosh Hashanah meal includes a round loaf of challah bread (center) topped with apples dipped in honey. Around the challah, from top left, are honey, fresh dates, pomegranates and an apple.

them from the judgment of God should they be unable to live up to the vows they make to themselves. (The recitation of the Kol Nidre does not change the fact that obligations toward other people must be upheld.) The cantor and the congregation then ask for forgiveness "for all the people of Israel, including strangers among them." This is interpreted as a plea for forgiveness for the entire world, Jews ("the people of Israel") and non-Jews ("strangers") alike. By now the sun has gone down and Yom Kippur has begun. The evening service concludes with a long series of *selichot* prayers that express penance for sins.

On the morning of Yom Kippur, believers attend prayer services where they continue to recite the *selichot* prayers begun the previous evening. Afternoon prayers include a reading from the book of Jonah that emphasizes God's forgiveness of those who repent their sins. Yom Kippur ends after sundown, when the shofar is blown. The shofar has great significance in the Torah. Ancient Jews played shofars in processions and as they marched into battle. Religious leaders used shofars to announce holidays, new Moons, and other special events. Rosh Hashanah begins with the sound of a shofar to tell people that the time has come to seek forgiveness. On Yom Kippur, it signals the end of the fast and of the High Holy Days. After the service people are free to eat. Many Jews share a snack at the synagogue with other worshippers, such as honey, apples, and challah, the traditional braided, egg-rich bread. They then return home for a large meal with their families.

Rains Retreat

Rains Retreat, or Vassa, is a Buddhist holiday celebrated from July to October, around the time some parts of Asia experience an intense rainy season. It is often referred to as "the Buddhist Lent." Though such a label does not portray the holiday in all of its complexity, there is some truth to the comparison. Like Lent and Yom Kippur, Rains Retreat is a time of renewal, repentance, and preparation for the year ahead. It also follows the model of the Buddha, who spent time in the forest during the rainy season after his enlightenment. It is an important holiday both for Buddhist monks and laypeople, those who are not monks but who follow closely the beliefs and practices of a given religion.

The Origins of Rains Retreat

Buddhism

Buddhism is an ancient religion founded in the late sixth century B.C.E. by Siddhartha Gautama. Siddhartha was born in India to wealthy parents. He had all the worldly pleasures life could offer. As he got older, however, he began to notice the inequality between his life and the lives of those around him. This

Buddhist monks pray in Laos during the observance of Rains Retreat, which lasts through the rainy season.

led him to renounce almost all of his material possessions. He left his wife and son to lead a life of simplicity and humility. After a period of time spent living in the wilderness, he began to meditate on the nature of existence.

During one of these meditations he attained a state of divine knowledge known as enlightenment or nirvana. In this state he felt the truth of life had been revealed to him. He believed that, through meditation, he had found the answers to suffering and how to achieve a permanent release from it. Siddhartha believed that a person's actions in the present determine how his or her life will be in the future. This is known as karma. Someone who acts in a fair and kind manner throughout his or her life is said to have good karma. Siddhartha also believed that those with good karma are closer to enlightenment than those with bad karma. Through a process of reincarnation, or rebirth in a new form after death, one may come continually closer to enlightenment. With every new life is a chance to attain enlightenment, and thus to free oneself from the endless suffering of the world.

After attaining enlightenment, Siddhartha proclaimed himself the Buddha ("The Enlightened One") and began to spread his knowledge so that others could also free themselves from life's burdens. The Buddha began to roam the countryside of India and present-day Nepal sharing what he had discovered. He attracted many followers but stressed that he was not a spiritual leader. Rather, he claimed that the ability to attain enlightenment was within everyone, available for his or her own discovery.

When Buddha started to preach, the most important doctrines he taught were the Four Noble Truths and the Eightfold Path. The first of the Noble Truths is that suffering is inevitable and almost universal through loss, failure, pain, and the temporary nature of pleasures. The second Noble Truth is that attachment to the things of this world and the desire to possess them causes suffering. The third Noble Truth gives hope. It says that the end of all suffering can be obtained through nirvana, a state of consciousness reached when the mind achieves complete liberation and detachment from desire or any kind of craving. The last of the Four Noble Truths teaches that, in order to end suffering, practitioners have to follow the Eightfold Path.

The Eightfold Path includes right views, right intention, right speech, right action, right livelihood, right endeavor, right mindfulness, and right concentration. The right views are the understanding of the Four Noble Truths. Right intention refers to following the right path in life. Right speech means not to condemn, lie, criticize, gossip, or use insensitive language. Right action involves following the Five Precepts, which are similar to the biblical Ten Commandments. Right livelihood means supporting oneself without harming others. It is followed by right endeavor, which requires making an effort to promote good thoughts. The seventh path is right mindfulness, or becoming aware of one's body, mind, and feelings. The last element of the Eightfold Path is right concentration, or meditation, a mental state in which one can achieve the highest level of consciousness.

Mahayana Buddhism

As the years progressed, Buddhist monasteries and temples working independently of one another began to develop their own interpretations of the Buddha's teachings. In the northern part of Asia, Buddhists in countries including China, Tibet, Korea, and Japan believed the religion needed to be altered to accommodate the needs of laypeople. They felt the demands of Buddhist practice, which included strenuous fasting, prolonged periods of meditation, and isolation from the family were too harsh for the average man or woman. This would make it difficult for them to attain enlightenment. Since the Buddha taught that everyone could and should be allowed to find the enlightenment within them, the Buddhists in these places made the religion more adaptable to the daily lives of non-monks. For example, meditation was not a requirement to attaining nirvana. Laypeople could attain this state through good works and love of the Buddha. This school of Buddhism became known as Mahayana Buddhism.

Theravada Buddhism

Other monasteries in the southern part of Asia, including Sri Lanka, India, Cambodia, Laos, and Thailand, were less willing to alter Buddhist doctrines to fit the lives of laypeople. They strove to keep the monastic tradition as the surest path to enlightenment. The emphasis was placed on rigorous discipline of the mind and body and the need to perfect one's karma. Love of the Buddha alone was not enough to attain nirvana. One had to follow as closely as possible the actual practices of the Buddha. This school of Buddhism was first known as Hinayana Buddhism. Today only one branch of this school remains, called Theravada Buddhism. It is important to note that only Theravada Buddhists celebrate Rains Retreat. Mahayana Buddhists have long seen the holiday as archaic and irrelevant, in keeping with their

A Cambodian woman holds incense sticks and prays at a Buddhist temple in Phnom Penh during Rains Retreat.

custom of casting off traditions they consider outdated to adapt Buddhism to modern times. Mahayana communities were formed in regions without significant rainy seasons. Thus they had less of a need to adopt the tradition.

Buddha's Travels and the Development of Rains Retreat

To this day, certain parts of Asia where the Buddha traveled are subject to an intense rainy season. This season lasts approximately three months, from August to October. Heavy winds called monsoons blow storm clouds in from the sea, drenching the landscape with water. It is said that the Buddha spent the first rainy season after his enlightenment deep in the forests of India. Here, sheltered from the storms, he continued to meditate, pray, and refine his knowledge. This was to become the model for the holiday of Rains Retreat. The Buddha further defined the holiday when he ordered his disciples not to travel during the rainy season as a way to avoid killing insects and crops. The Buddha's followers were largely spread out throughout the countryside following his death (ca. 480 B.C.E.) They wandered individually, begging for food and sleeping outdoors. Over time the early Buddhists began to gather into small communities. During the monsoon season, these communities would retreat to the woods in imitation of the Buddha. Here they would renew their commitment to uphold his teachings in an environment of mutual support.

In the next few centuries after the Buddha's death, Buddhism began to spread across the Asian continent. More and more laypeople became interested in the religion. To deepen their understanding, they made contact with the monastic communities scattered throughout the region. Many donated food, clothing, or other necessities to the monks, as well as money to construct housing. The result of this was that the monastic communities were able to build the first Buddhist monasteries, known as *viharas*, for use during their yearly retreats. It was in these monasteries that the practices of Buddhism were standardized and its holy texts compiled into a series of books called the Pali canon. Pali is the ancient Indian language in which many of these texts were written.

Observing Rains Retreat

Like Yom Kippur, the dates for Rains Retreat are based on the lunar calendar, a way of tracking time by the movements of the Moon around Earth. Rains Retreat lasts from the eighth to the 11th lunar month. Each of these months is about 29 days on the solar Gregorian calendar, corresponding to the months of late July through October.

Getting Ready for Rains Retreat

Around three weeks before Rains Retreat, monks are allowed to leave their monasteries to visit their families. They know they will be confined to their monasteries for the next three months, so many take full advantage of this opportunity. Buses are filled and travel is often slow during this period due to all the men returning home.

The day before Rains Retreat is known as Asalha Puja. It commemorates the day of the Buddha's first public sermon following his enlightenment. On Asalha Puja, Buddhists go to their local temple or monastery to make donations, hear sermons, and study texts. Sometimes on this day members of the laity, or lay community, take vows to improve themselves or more diligently support their local monastery and then join the monks for Rains Retreat. This is a fairly common practice that many people do every year as a way of renewing their Buddhist faith.

Rains Retreat: Wan Kao Pansa

Rains Retreat officially begins the day after Asalha Puja. This is called Wan Kao Pansa, which means, "to enter the residence period." From this point on, all inhabitants of the monastery—both monks and laypeople who have taken temporary vows—are not allowed to leave. Friends and family may bring further donations in the morning, often including

A group of Buddhist monks in Bangkok, Thailand, receive an offering of food on the first day of Rains Retreat.

candles, but once they are gone there is very little contact for the rest of the holiday. Until October the monks will devote themselves to meditation and spiritual training. They will help the laity understand the concepts of Buddhism, indoctrinate young monks, and study scripture. They will often give up bad habits, foods, or other obstacles in the way of a healthy spiritual life. These sacrifices are totally self-administered. That is, there is no authority figure or religious teaching that tells what to give up and for how long. It is instead a personal decision based on one's own spiritual needs.

There are few specific customs of Rains Retreat. Unlike Lent or Yom Kippur, for example, it is a different holiday from monastery to monastery. It depends on the interests of the community, who is present, and proscribed practices. Since it is a largely self-directed holiday, the only constant is the atmosphere of intense contemplation of Buddhist beliefs. One shared custom is the *pavarana* ceremony at the end of the three-month period. During this ceremony, all monks in residence make themselves open to criticism from all other monks. No one takes a position of authority, and everyone must be willing to accept the suggestions of others. It is a way of showing humility as well as breaking down the traditional barriers between students and teachers. A second ceremony called *kathina* takes place the following month. Here, laypeople who took vows to make the retreat give gifts to the monks as a way of thanking them for their hospitality and for sharing their experience.

Harmony Between and Within

Atonement days and rituals give people a chance to reset and renew. Almost every culture known has formal, sometimes ceremonial, ways of having people make amends and reparations. On the days of atonement, people are given the opportunity to ask for forgiveness, and create a better future by improving upon the past. They often emerge from this process feeling uplifted and revitalized.

A rabbi reads from the Hebrew holy book, the Torah, at a Mississippi synagogue on Yom Kippur.

Regional Traditions and Customs

◎ ◎ ◎

Africa

Lent in Africa

Christianity has a long history in Africa. The religion spread through North Africa and Ethiopia starting in the first and second centuries C.E. The people of sub-Saharan Africa practiced indigenous religions (local religions derived from their native cultures) until European missionaries arrived in the 1700s and 1800s and began converting Africans to Christianity. Between 1900 and 2000 Christianity gained in popularity. In 1900 only about 10 million Africans were Christian, but by 2000 about 350 million Africans, about 47 percent of the population of the continent, practiced Christian religions.

Christians celebrating the festival of Palm Sunday, known locally as Rameaux, parade through the streets of Guiglo in western Côte d'Ivoire.

Not all African Christians observe Lent. About half of Africa's Christians are fairly recent converts to evangelical churches that do not follow older Christian traditions. However, there are still a number of Roman Catholics, Anglicans, and members of other Christian denominations that observe Lent throughout Africa. For example, about 26 percent of Nigeria's approximately 51 million Christians are of Protestant faiths, while 14 percent are Roman Catholic. Sixty-two percent of the population of Cape Verde is Roman Catholic. Even in North Africa, in which Islam is by far the most widely held faith, there is a significant Christian population. The largest group of Christians in North Africa is the Coptic Christians of Egypt who make up about 9 percent of the more than 80,330,000 people living there.

African Catholics and Protestants who observe Lent follow most of the practices of their churches. These include going to church on Ash Wednesday to receive the traditional mark of ashes on their foreheads, avoiding eating meat on Fridays, and giving up bad habits and other overindulgences. During Holy Week, the last week of Lent, African Christians go to church more than usual. They attend Palm Sunday services and participate in processions carrying palm fronds. On Good Friday, many people attend religious services to commemorate the day of Jesus' death and crucifixion. Good Friday is a public holiday in Nigeria. Passion plays and Stations of the Cross ceremonies are also very popular.

Yom Kippur in Africa

There are few Jews in Africa. Until the late 18th and early 19th centuries there were fairly large communities of Sephardic Jews in North Africa (Jews whose ancestors lived in Spain; in this case many of them moved to North Africa in the 1400s), but most have long since immigrated to other countries, particularly the United States, France, Spain, and Israel. Many of them left because of the increase of anti-Semitism in their homelands, especially before, during, and after World War II (1939–1945). A few Jews still live in Morocco and Tunisia and observe the Yom Kippur rituals.

A group of Jews called the Beta Israel has lived in Ethiopia since the third century but most of them immigrated to Israel in the 20th century. Only a few thousand Jews still live in Ethiopia. A number of African groups consider themselves to be Jewish or observe rituals that seem Jewish. According to their own oral legends, the Jews of Nigeria believe they migrated from Israel and have been living in Africa for about 1,500 years. Experts estimate that about 40,000 Jews live in Nigeria.

Zimbabwe's Jewish community is so small that it must fly in a rabbi from South Africa to lead Yom Kippur services. At its height, Zimbabwe's Jewish population was about 7,000 strong. In recent years, however, most of them have left the country and only a few hundred are left there today.

The largest African Jewish community is in South Africa. There are two major groups who contributed to the size of the community. These are the Ashkenazi (eastern European) and Russian Jews who fled eastern Europe during the 19th century. Many of them settled in Cape Town, a large city in South Africa. Their community grew throughout the early part of the 20th century. Yom Kippur was a major holiday for them. Jews from surrounding areas would travel miles to attend Yom Kippur services in Cape Town. Jewish businesses closed down and believers fasted together from sunset to sunset. By the 1960s there were more than 100,000 Jews in South Africa. After this point, however, the population began to decline as descendants of these Jews stopped practicing their religion. By 1974 so few Jews were practicing in the area that the synagogue in Cape Town was made into a museum of Jewish heritage.

Today there about 70,000 Jews left in South Africa, the vast majority of them living in the city of Johannesburg. Hundreds of Jews leave the country every year, so the population is shrinking. Of those that remain there are a number of observant Jews. Holidays such as Yom Kippur bring them together. African Jews observe most of the same Yom Kippur rituals as Jews elsewhere: asking forgiveness, eating a large meal on Erev Yom Kippur, and spending the holiday in fasting and prayer.

Unique Traditions and Customs
Breaking Fast with Chicken Stew in Algeria

Christians and Jews make up about 1 percent of the population (Algeria is 99 percent Muslim). Chicken is the traditional Yom Kippur meat in Algeria and other countries in North Africa because so many chickens are killed during the ritual sacrifice of *kapparot*. North African families often prepare their post-fast meal the day before Yom Kippur, making dishes that can be easily reheated. Chicken stew with chickpeas, chicken with couscous (a type of cereal made of semolina flour), fried chicken with egg-plant, and a vegetable stew called *harira* are all popular Yom Kippur feast dishes. In Algeria, people also make a rich egg bread flavored with anise.

Lent in Cameroon

The country of Cameroon is one of great contrasts for its relatively small size. Approximately 40 percent of the country is Christian, 40 percent practices indigenous beliefs, and the remaining 20 percent are Muslim. Of the Christian population, the majority is Roman Catholic—4.25 million people, or 26 percent of the total population. Due to the large missionary presence within the country, it is among the Catholic community that Lent is celebrated with the greatest fervor in Cameroon. Priests and missionaries alike lead believers in Lenten fasts, prayer groups, and other activities that resemble spiritual retreats. On Good Friday, devout Christians attend special church services that focus on the life and teachings of Jesus. Choirs singing hymns are a highlight of the celebrations while plays based on Jesus' life are also staged. In Cameroon, some faithful Christians fast on Good Friday. When they eat, it is usually fish instead of meat. In addition to attracting the people of Cameroon, many outsiders are drawn to visit the country during their Lenten pilgrimage.

Lent in Chad

In Chad the majority of the population is Muslim (about 51 percent). The next largest percentage of the population is Christian (about 35 percent). During Lent Chadian Christians attend prayer services, and the life and teachings of Jesus are remembered. In bigger towns special communal Good Friday services are held and attended by thousands of people. The service is followed by cross-bearing processions that imitate Jesus' last journey.

Consumption of meat, alcohol, and other indulgences are strictly prohibited during the 40 days' fasting of Lent. Many people also fast on Good Friday, while others eat a light meal. It is a day filled with sadness. Gospel readings and plays showcasing the life of Jesus are a regular feature during Holy Week in Chad.

Lent in Egypt

Copts fast the week before Lent begins and during the six weeks of the Great Lent, as it is called in Orthodox churches. On fast days, they do not eat meat, fish, eggs, or dairy products. Devout Copts perform an even stricter fast during Holy Week, eating and drinking nothing at all between midnight and sunset. People who find this too difficult may eat nothing between midnight and noon. Fasting is most important on the Friday before Easter, called Great Friday.

Coptic Christian priests take part in a midnight service to celebrate Christ's resurrection, at the Coptic Cathedral in Cairo, Egypt. The Coptic Church is the native Christian church of Egypt, and has a doctrine similar to Greek Orthodox and Russian Orthodox churches.

Lent in Equatorial Guinea

The third-smallest country in Africa by population, Equatorial Guinea is predominantly Christian with 93 percent of its inhabitants following the Christian faith. Of these 87 percent are Roman Catholic. Like its neighbor, Cameroon, such high percentages can be attributed to the great deal of missionary activity within the country, both in the past and the present day. In Equatorial Guinea devout Catholics attend a special Good Friday Mass. The life and teachings of Jesus are remembered, and devotional hymns are sung.

Lent in Ethiopia

Ethiopia is home to a unique Christian church, the Ethiopian Orthodox Church. The Ethiopian Orthodox Church has long been isolated from the rest of the Christian churches, and it has developed some of its own traditions. Thirty-five to 40 percent of Ethiopia is Ethiopian Christian.

Ethiopian Orthodox Christians observe a particularly strict fast during Lent. Lent for them lasts 55 days. They avoid eating meat and dairy products during this time. Instead they concentrate on vegetarian foods such as grains, lentils, split peas, vegetable stews, and fruit, which they serve with a flat spongy pancake called *injera*. On weekdays during Lent, many people do not eat at all until about 3 P.M. On Saturdays and Sundays, they are allowed to eat a meal after the morning service in addition to the afternoon meal. Ethiopian Christians end Lent by going to church on the evening before Easter. The service lasts until after midnight, after which everyone goes home to eat a meal made from chicken or lamb that was slaughtered the previous evening. Children stay up late for this meal.

Yom Kippur in Ethiopia

Although most of the Beta Israel Jews of Ethiopia left the country to move to Israel in the late 20th century, a few Jews remain in Ethiopia's capital, Addis Ababa, and along the border with Sudan to the west. The Beta Israel based their rituals directly on the Torah, which means they follow a slightly different calendar from mainstream Jews. During Yom Kippur, they fast from sunset to sunset, spending most of the day in the *mesgid*, or synagogue. Beta Israel synagogues contain stone altars used for sacrificing animals. The religious leaders, called *cahenats*, conduct Yom Kippur sacrifices at which they kill animals as the Torah prescribes. The *cahenats* claim to be descended from Moses' brother Aaron. The people say prayers in Ge'ez, an Ethiopian language.

Lent in Lesotho

The major portion of Lesotho lies on a highland: the Karoo Basin. The terrain is made up of mostly hills, plateaus, and mountains. Lesotho is unique in that all of South Africa encircles it—Lestho is completely enclosed by mountains that separate it from South Africa. Twenty percent of Lesotho's population follow indigenous beliefs and the remaining 80 percent classify themselves as Christian. While the majority of these Christians are Roman Catholic, various evangelical and other Protestant denominations account for a significant number as well. On Good Friday Christians in Lesotho attend church, sing hymns, and pray. The life of Jesus is remembered through enacting plays and singing devotional songs. People also conduct processions to reenact Jesus' last journey to Calvary. Most observe a partial fast.

The Ashkenazi of Mozambique

Mozambique's capital city, Maputo, has been home to a small community of European Jews since the late 1800s. The city's synagogue was built in 1926. The Jewish community reached its largest population, about 500, during the 1940s, as Jews fleeing from Europe settled in Africa. After the nation became independent from Portugal in 1975, however, years of civil war drove many of the country's Jews away. Today there are only about 20 Jews in Maputo, and they only occasionally gather in the synagogue. Yom Kippur is a very subdued holiday, observed largely in private by Mozambique's remaining Jews.

Lent in Nigeria

Forty percent of the Nigerian population is Christian. Nigerian Christians attend Good Friday services in their local churches. Politicians also deliver special Good Friday speeches and call upon Nigerians to emulate the model values of love and sacrifice demonstrated by Jesus. In 2008, the day's events included a mock crucifixion where an actor was physically strapped to a cross to reenact Jesus' suffering. Other Nigerian Christians held several processions in which they carried around large crucifixes to draw peoples' attention to Christ's sacrifice.

Yom Kippur in Nigeria

Nigeria is also home to a small community of Jews called the Igbo Jews, or the Ibo Benei-Yesrael. These Jews claim that their ancestors came to Nigeria back in the seventh century after the destruction of the First and Second Temples in Jerusalem. On Yom Kippur, these Jews observe the traditional practice—they bathe before the start of the holiday to remove uncleanness, they fast from sunset to sunset, and they attend Hebrew services in one of the nation's synagogues.

Lent in Senegal

In Senegal, one of the most Islamized nations in West Africa, Christianity is followed by only 5 percent of the population. Most Christians are Roman Catholics, who number about half a million. Many Senegalese Roman Catholics do not eat or drink at all during daylight hours throughout Lent. Instead they eat one meal a day after sunset. Senegal is primarily Muslim, and this is the type of fast that Muslims observe during the holy Islamic month of Ramadan. Senegalese Catholics influenced by the Muslim community have applied this custom to their own Lenten practice.

Lent in Uganda

About 66 percent of Uganda's population is Christian. During Lent, Ugandan Christians attend prayer services in church and reflect on Jesus' life and teachings. Choirs sing devotional songs, and plays based on the life of Jesus are performed as part of the solemn Good Friday observance. In some parts of Uganda Christians walk in huge processions, some carrying crosses, reenacting Jesus' final journey to Calvary.

Asia

Rains Retreat in Asia

The majority of the world's 350 million Buddhists live on the continent of Asia. Those of the Mahayana school are located mostly in the northern countries of China, South Korea, and Japan. Theravada Buddhists are based largely in the southern countries, including Sri Lanka, India, Cambodia, Laos, Thailand, and Myanmar. As only Theravada Buddhists celebrate Rains Retreat, it is primarily the southern countries that have established the holiday's particular traditions, though the Mahayana Buddhists of Bhutan in Central Asia observe an event similar to Rains Retreat.

Rains Retreat is not an official government holiday in southern Asia, primarily because it takes place over such an extended period of time. The public's participation in the holiday is confined to the Wan Kao Pansa, its first official day and the anniversary of the Buddha's first public sermon. On this day men and women from surrounding towns will come to their local monastery or temple and donate food, clothing, and candles. They will stay to listen to sermons and pray or meditate with the monks. Throughout the holiday, these same local people may choose to come back for short stays at the monastery to participate in meditation sessions and spiritual training.

Lent in Asia

Christianity exists throughout Asia, but in most countries Christians are a distinct minority. The main exceptions are the Philippines and East Timor. These countries are predominantly Roman Catholic due to the fact that they were colonized by Spain and Portugal, Roman Catholic countries. In the 1500 and 1600s many Spanish and Portuguese people, especially Catholic priests who came as missionaries, moved to those countries and converted the people to Christianity. There are a number of Catholics in South Korea (about 7 percent) and Vietnam (about 6 percent) as well. Most other Asian countries, including China and India, also have Christian communities.

In most of Asia, Ash Wednesday, Good Friday, and Maundy Thursday are not official holidays, so Christians must go to school or work as

Churchgoers wave palm fronds during Mass on Palm Sunday at a church in Manila, Philippines. Palm Sunday is one of the high points in the observance of Lent in this largely Roman Catholic country.

usual. Believers who observe Lent do not have many public outlets to practice their religion other than their church. They participate in activities on Palm Sunday, Good Friday, and Holy Saturday. They may also go to confession or participate in a Stations of the Cross ceremony. The exception to this is the Philippines, where Lent is a major event that can be the focus of entire communities. Some towns hold festivals that last for many days in which townspeople of all ages reenact the events of Jesus' life.

A Muslim boy lights a candle at a graveyard during Shab-i-Barat in Bangladesh. Muslims visit ancestral graveyards praying for the salvation of the souls of the departed. They also believe that all sins will be forgiven by praying to Allah throughout the Shab-i Barat night.

Shab-i Barat in South Asia

Many South Asian Muslims, particularly in India, Pakistan, and Bangladesh, celebrate Shab-i Barat, the Muslim day of atonement. The festival takes place 15 days before the beginning of Ramadan. A whole night of prayer is devoted to asking for forgiveness for the past year and for good fortune in the year to come. People share dishes such as stews and curries, and distribute sweets among friends and relatives to celebrate the day.

Yom Kippur in Asia

There are small groups of Jews living all over Asia. Until the 1990s, communities of Bukharian Jews lived in Central Asia, but almost all of them left the country after the fall of the Soviet Union and moved to the United States, Israel, Europe, and Australia.

Jews have lived in China since at least the eighth century C.E., although they may have been there five centuries earlier. Some Jews moved to China to escape the Holocaust in Europe in the 1930s and 1940s. About 20,000 Jews were believed to live in Shanghai in 1941. However, the majority of Chinese Jews gave up their religious practices during the 20th century.

There are three main Jewish communities in India. The Cochinis and the Bene Israel consider themselves to be descendants of the Lost Ten Tribes of Israel, who came to India long before the birth of Jesus. The Baghdadis are descendants of Jews who came to India from Iraq in the early 1800s. These Indian Jews have lived peacefully with Indians of other religions for centuries. They have historically dressed in Indian clothing, used Hindu names, and spoken local languages, so it is impossible to distinguish them from their fellow Indians based on casual observation. They have, however, kept up Jewish religious practices such as circumcision (cutting away of the male foreskin) and dietary laws. Most of India's Jews immigrated to Israel during the 20th century. There are only about 5,000 Jews living in India today.

Most Jews living in Asia today observe modern Jewish practices. On Yom Kippur they may give money to charity, eat a big meal before the start of the holiday, and attend services at a synagogue. Some practices can be difficult to observe. For example, not all Jews in Asia have access to a traditional *mikvah*, so it is not always possible for them to take the ritual bath. Jews who do not live near a synagogue cannot easily attend services, and some Jews are not allowed to take the day off from work. It can also be difficult to fast when other people are eating. Still, many Jews living in Asia do the best they can to observe Yom Kippur.

Unique Traditions and Customs
Atonement in Bangladesh

In Bangladesh, where Muslims compose more than 80 percent of the population, Shab-i Barat, the Muslim day of atonement or night of forgiveness, is an official holiday. Falling just in advance of Ramadan, it is the night on which Allah writes down the fate of all people for the coming year. People pray for forgiveness for past deeds and for prosperity as they prepare for the sacred month ahead. The holiday has a social element in that the faithful may dress formally and visit with friends, delivering sweets and asking forgiveness, and praying for one another. Shab-i Barat also occasions charity to the poor and visits to ancestral graves.

Muslim children light candles for Shab-i Barat in Bangladesh. Shab-i Barat is a Muslim holy night marked by special prayers seeking good fortune and forgiveness.

Nothing Like a Rainy Day in Bhutan

Seventy-five percent of the population of Bhutan is Buddhist and at the end of the rainy season, people in Bhutan celebrate a holiday related to Rains Retreat known as "Blessed Rainy Day." It takes place during September of the Gregorian calendar. On this day, legend has it that female celestial beings called *khandroms* shower blessings onto Earth in the form of rain. The rain washes away any bad luck and cleanses the landscape. People honor this day by showering and washing their hair. This ritual symbolically renews their bodies and souls.

Curfews in East Timor

East Timor gained independence from Indonesia in 2002. About 90 percent of its population is Roman Catholic. The country has been in a state of unrest for several years. In 2008, the nation was subject to a curfew during Lent in order to prevent violent attacks on political leaders following a number of assassination and coup attempts. The government relaxed this curfew during Holy Week so that Catholics could participate in Lenten activities. On Good Friday, Christians in East Timor fast all day. Traditionally the reenactment of Jesus' procession to the place where he was crucified was also an important annul ritual. Catholic Timorese generally spend the day in devotion, listening to public readings of Gospels and Psalms and singing hymns. Nighttime vigils are held on Easter Eve.

The Bene Israel Jews of India

Because they were isolated from other Jews for so many centuries, the Jews of India have developed some unique Yom Kippur customs. The Bene Israel have traditionally called Yom Kippur *Durfalnicha san*, which means "the festival of closing the doors." The day before Yom Kippur, believers clean themselves in a ritual called *malma*, bathing in hot and cold water. Many Bene Israel Jews did

A father holds his daughter as a rabbi (right) recites a prayer at a synagogue in Mumbai, India, during Yom Kippur.

not traditionally use a *mikvah* for ritual cleansing. Instead they washed themselves in ordinary tap water.

On Yom Kippur, they dress in white, take off their shoes, and lock themselves in their houses from 5 P.M. until 7 P.M. the following day. They pray, fast, and avoid all contact with non-Jews. In the past, neighbors of Bene Israel Jews would take care of their livestock while they were locked in their houses. The believers used to then conclude the holiday by having young people pay homage to their elders and wives pay homage to their husbands by kneeling at their feet, but this is not a common custom anymore.

Atonement in India

Muslims in India—about 13 percent of the population—also observe Shab-i Barat, the Muslim day of atonement. In Rajasthan, a large section of India that borders Pakistan, people observe Shab-i Barat by kneeling and praying all night, offering their tears in exchange for forgiveness. The next day, sweets are handed out among friends and relatives. These treats along with special blessings are said to ease the pains of life. In Madhya Pradesh, an area in the center of India, women enjoy a separate set of celebrations, reciting parts of the Quran and telling mythical stories.

Challah and Cholent in Japan

Kobe, Japan, is home to a population of about 70 Jews who come from many different countries, including the United States, Canada, Israel, Syria, Iran, and Morocco. They are what remains of a larger population of Jews that lived in Japan since the 1860s. The community attracts regular visits from Jews passing through the area. Orthodox Jews and rabbis from New York occasionally visit to help conduct services. Traveling families visit the synagogue on holy days and especially on Yom Kippur. The participants maintain Orthodox Jewish practices and try to serve Jewish foods on holidays. A post–Yom Kippur meal can include traditional European and American Jewish foods such as challah bread, cholent (a type of stew), salad, wine, and beer. It may also feature Japanese rice, fish, soy sauce, and other local ingredients.

Bouk Khao Phansa in Laos

In Laos, Rains Retreat is known as Bouk Khao Phansa. Young men who wish to become monks will often wait until Rains Retreat to make their profession. This is a symbolic gesture, as they feel they are beginning their journey toward enlightenment during the most focused and disciplined part of the Buddhist year. Some men will remain monks only for a short period of time, then leave the monastery to marry or pursue other things. They see the monastic profession more as a duty and a way to honor their parents than as a lifetime commitment.

At the conclusion of Bouk Khao Phansa, local laypeople visit the monasteries bearing gifts for the monks. On the evening of the final day, a beautiful ceremony known as Lua Hai Fai takes place. In this ceremony, people fashion small boats out of banana leaves and fill them with things such as incense and candles. The boats are then floated down rivers as offerings to the monks.

Lights and Dancing in Myanmar

On the day before the end of Rains Retreat in Myanmar, Buddhists (about 90 percent of the population) adorn their homes and streets with candles and electric lights. They do this because they believe the Buddha spends the Rains Retreat among celestial beings teaching a sermon called the *Abhidamma*. The lights are a way of welcoming him back to Earth. They recall the ladder of stars on which he descends from the heavens along with his disciples. In cities and towns across the country, the streets are filled with live music, dance groups, and food stalls. Young people offer gifts to their elders as a way of marking the occasion.

Pilgrims worship at a sacred pagoda in Yangon, Myanmar, during Rains Retreat. Nearly 90 percent of Myanmar's population practices Buddhism.

Lent in the Philippines

Devout Catholics in the Philippines (which is about 81 percent Roman Catholic) sometimes take the penitential side of Lent to an extreme. Penitents, or people who confess their sins in order to be forgiven, occasionally engage in acts that seem extreme or even dangerous. This behavior goes far beyond the typical Lenten sacrifice or fasting. Some Catholics in the Philippines whip their own backs until they bleed. Whipping is also called "flagellation." Flagellation was a common form of penance in Europe several centuries ago. Spanish Catholic missionaries brought it to the Philippines in the 16th and 17th centuries. At that time, it was considered a demonstration not only of experiencing some of the tortures Christ endured but also as a symbol of the spirit triumphing over physical pain.

Two centuries after the Spaniards introduced self-flagellation to the Philippines, the Catholic Church began to prohibit it. Missionaries considered it an anachronism, or something that belonged to the past. Though interest and practice died down, there were still locations where the custom continued, especially in the rural countryside.

On Maundy Thursday, Filipino Christians carry crosses reenacting the sufferings of Jesus Christ in the belief that it will atone for their sins.

In the 1950s flagellation revived and gathered momentum, following the independence of the Philippines from colonial rule. In the 1960s, the first reenactment of the Crucifixion took place after a man who had practiced flagellation decided he wanted to be crucified to be closer to God. Today, both practices of flagellation and mock crucifixion are much a part of the Filipino Catholic Lent.

It is commonly accepted that the participants reenact the Crucifixion in order to atone for sins. Social anthropologists who have studied the self-flagellations and crucifixions, especially in their historical context, have found that this is not the true motivation. Prior to the arrival of Christianity, religious beliefs in the Philippines did not contain concepts such as sin, atonement, hell, or punishment for sin. Nor did Filipinos make religious vows. What the anthropologists have discovered is that the majority of young men who undergo flagellation and/or crucifixion do so as a sacrifice for a sick relative or friend. Usually the vows are made during a time of crisis, often related to the illness of a loved one. These young men hope that by undertaking such a sacrifice, healing will be given to the person close to them, and their entire family will be protected or benefited in some way.

Moriones Festival in the Philippines

The Moriones Festival on the small Philippine island of Marinduque is one of the largest Lenten festivals in the Philippines. The towns of the island turn themselves into living stages to enact a weeklong play about the search for Longinus, the Roman centurion who pierced Jesus' side with a spear as he hung on the cross. According to tradition, Longinus was blind in one eye. After he stabbed Jesus, the blood from Jesus' side fell on his eye and miraculously restored his sight. He converted to Christianity, much to the displeasure of his fellow Roman soldiers.

The festival begins on Holy Monday. Throughout the week, costumed men walk the streets wearing *morions*, the visors that ancient Roman soldiers wore on their helmets. The men participate in the festival as a means of atoning for sins. They finally find Longinus on the day before Easter and capture him. On Easter they pretend to cut off his head as punishment for betraying Rome's pagan gods by converting to Christianity. Tourists come from all over the country to watch this event. Boats are sometimes overloaded with the crowds of people traveling to the small island. Other popular events in Marinduque include the Way of the Cross, processions of flagellants whipping their own backs, and recitations of the story of the

Filipino children wearing colorful wooden masks and dressed as Roman guards walk down the streets in a town in the Philippines. The penitence, locally known as Moriones, is an annual ritual in the predominantly Roman Catholic country in which residents remember the suffering of Jesus Christ during Lent.

Passion called the *pabasa*. Villages also enact stage plays about the life and death of Jesus called *cenaculos*.

Lent in Thailand

Though Thailand is about 95 percent Buddhist, there are Catholics in Thailand who often participate in retreats during Lent. A retreat can last a day, a weekend, a week, or longer. Some of these retreats are completely silent. Television, radios, music players, cell phones, and computers are banned. Other retreats are partially silent, but include time to pray and talk together about spirituality and the meaning of Lent. Lenten retreats in Thailand often end with a Stations of the Cross. Some Protestants also participate in retreats during Lent.

Rains Retreat in Thailand

Like other celebrants of Rains Retreat, Thai Buddhists use the holiday as a chance to reacquaint themselves with the teachings of the Buddha. Many will also use it as a "test period" in a monastery to see if they would like to pursue a monastic life. One of the most unique traditions, however, is the southeastern city of Ubon Ratchathani's Candle Festival.

To prepare for this festival, laypeople create candles of various sizes to give as donations to local monasteries. They are either carved directly from wax, or wood that is then coated with wax. Some of them can become quite large in size. Each candle represents a local temple or monastery, or

A Thai woman offers flowers to young Buddhist monks at a temple north of Bangkok in observance of Rains Retreat.

else features scenes of Buddhist history and mythology. On the morning of Wan Kao Pansa, the inaugural day of Rains Retreat, the candles are paraded through the streets of Ubon Ratchathani. Dancers and musicians accompany the parade. Though the candles are often too large to donate to monasteries, the tradition makes for an enjoyable way to enter the rigorous months of Rains Retreat.

A Resurgent Catholicism in Vietnam

Roman Catholics constitute about 6 percent of the population in Vietnam. Many of Vietnam's Catholics went many years without any formal religious services during the second half of the 20th century. Priests left the country during the Vietnam War (1959–75) and did not return for a long time. Although people in the cities returned to their traditional religious practices during the 1980s and 1990s, Catholics in remote regions had no priests until the early 2000s. Catholics who lived in northern Vietnam did not get to celebrate services for Holy Week, Good Friday, and Easter Sunday from 1963 until 2003, the year a priest finally visited them again. Some Catholics kept up their religious practices as best they could, praying on their own, but Catholics believe that priests are necessary to conduct certain rituals. For example, only priests can conduct the Eucharist, the ritual of sharing bread and wine that commemorates the Last Supper. Catholics also believe that they need priests to conduct baptisms, weddings, and the ritual of confessing sins and having them forgiven. The lack of priests meant that Vietnamese children could not prepare for their first Communion—the first time they received the Eucharist, which was traditionally during the Lent when they were seven years old. The return of the priests meant that Catholics young and old could finally resume their customs.

Europe

Lent in Europe

Christianity is by far the largest religion in Europe. Roman Catholicism predominates in Ireland, Spain, Portugal, France, Italy, and Poland. Protestantism is more common in England, Scotland, Wales, and the Scandinavian countries. Eastern Orthodox religions are predominant farther east, in the countries spanning from Greece to Russia.

Though most Europeans are nominally Christian, many do not practice any kind of religion at all. A fairly large percentage of Europeans say they do not believe in God. Many others consider themselves to be Christian, but do not go to church. In the Netherlands, for example, about 5 million people call themselves Catholics, yet only about 10 percent attend Mass every week. Despite the tendency of European people to become more secular and less religious, Lent is still an important season in much of the continent. Countries with high populations of Roman Catholics and Eastern Orthodox believers have the most noticeable practices.

Many European cities celebrate carnival two weeks before Lent. Carnival runs roughly from mid-January until Ash Wednesday. During this time Europeans hold wild parties.

The majority of European Christians no longer follow the fasting rules for Lent, although Roman Catholics in Germany, Spain, and Italy typically do not eat meat on Fridays during Lent. Instead, they eat fish dishes. Many of the European Christians who observe Lent try to make some sacrifice or change of habit during Lent. Some try to do good deeds, such as donating food to the poor or volunteering in a hospital. Others give up things such as television, alcohol, or chocolate. Kids might give

The Vatican

The Vatican is home to the pope, the leader of the Roman Catholic Church. Located in Rome, Italy, the Vatican is a popular destination for religious tourists during Lent. Many devout Americans travel to Rome to visit the Vatican during Holy Week.

Belarussians dance near a burning figure symbolizing winter during a carnival marking Maslenitsa, which translates as Pancake Week, an ancient weeklong celebration of saying goodbye to winter in downtown Minsk, Russia. Maslenitsa is a traditional carnival in Russia, Belarus, and Ukraine, which starts right before Lent.

up computer games. Some religious leaders have tried to make Lent more relevant to a modern world by suggesting different sacrifices.

During Holy Week, many Catholic churches bottle holy water and give it out to the people who attend services. Churches enact Stations of the Cross ceremonies, often leading processions outside around the church or town. On Good Friday, cities in Italy and Spain hold parades to commemorate Jesus' walk to his crucifixion. On Holy Saturday, many churches hold masses that start at midnight and last for hours. At these Easter vigils, believers await the resurrection of Jesus. They may then go home for a short rest, and return to church for the Easter morning Mass. The Easter morning Mass is usually short, to make up for the long service of the night before and to give people plenty of time to feast with their friends and families.

A Day to Dye

Many European Christians dye their Easter eggs during Holy Week. Good Friday is a popular day for doing this.

Yom Kippur in Europe

There were many Jews in Europe from the medieval period through the early part of the 20th century. Between 9 and 11 million Jews lived in Europe in the 1930s. Since World War II (1939–45), however, the number of Jews has declined considerably. Many Jews left the country before or after World War II, immigrating to the United States, Israel, or Australia. Six million others died in the Holocaust. About 1 million Jews live in Europe today, mostly in France, England, Russia, and Germany.

The holiday traditions of the former European Jewry have spread through the world and are practiced by the remaining Jewish population. In times past Jews living in European cities would get ready for Yom Kippur by performing the ritual of *kapparot,* in which believers would transfer their sins to a chicken and then sacrifice it. Men would visit a *mikvah* to take a bath before the holiday began. On the afternoon before Yom Kippur, a Jewish family would sit down to a large pre-fast meal. In eastern and central Europe, the traditional meal before Yom Kippur would be simple but filling. It often involved chicken because the custom of *kapparot* resulted in a surplus of fresh chicken meat on Yom Kippur. Typical pre-fast meals were chicken soup with matzo balls (dumplings made of matzo meal, the dust made by grinding up a flat bread called matzo), dumplings made of unleavened bread, or another kind of dumpling called *kreplach* stuffed with chicken. *Kreplach* resemble ravioli, in that they are a dough shell with meat inside. The reason to serve *kreplach* on Yom Kippur is that the dough covers its filling just as kindness should cover any strict judgment of other's sins or misdeeds. After eating, Jews would gather at the synagogue to say the Kol Nidre prayer and attend Yom Kippur services. They would not eat at all that night or all the next day. Fasting and praying would continue for the day of Yom Kippur, until the sound of the shofar signaled that the Sun had set. Once Yom Kippur was over, European Jews would eat a large meal that could include chicken soup, roast chicken, chopped herring, honeyed carrots, fruit compote, fresh fruit, sponge cake, and lemon tea.

Many Jews who live in Europe today still follow old traditions. They fast, pray, and ask forgiveness of one another just as Jews do in other parts of the world. However, fewer Jews today kill chickens in the *kapparot* ritual, and many modern Jews have relaxed some of the stricter rules. Young European Jews, for example, may not spend the whole day of Yom Kippur fasting, and not all Jews can make it to a *mikvah* to take a ritual bath.

A Sweet Future

In European Jewish tradition, honeyed carrots bring good fortune and wealth because they resemble bright gold coins. The honey is supposed to make the future sweet.

Unique Traditions and Customs

A Centuries-Old Passion Play in Germany

Germany is famous for its elaborate Carnival celebrations and masked balls. Once Lent arrives, popular dishes include trout stuffed with sauerkraut, smoked trout and potato salad, and salmon stew. In Germany, some families collect all their candy when Lent begins and put it in a bowl. No one is supposed to touch it until Easter. This can be very difficult for children.

Germany is also home to one of the most famous passion plays in the world, the Oberammergau Passion Play, performed by the inhabitants of Oberammergau, Bavaria. Back in 1632, the residents of Oberammergau were struck with the bubonic plague, a deadly disease. They promised that if God would spare them, they would perform a passion play every 10 years. By 1633 people had stopped dying and the people decided that God had indeed spared them. The next year they kept their promise and put on a play depicting the last events in Jesus' life. They have continued to perform the play approximately every 10 years since then. Their next performance takes place in 2010. The modern performances involve more than 2,000 performers, including local children who play villagers in crowd scenes. They attract visitors from all over the world; since 1930, each passion play has attracted around 500,000 spectators. The performance includes music; dramatic readings of biblical passages; and tableaux, scenes in which silent and motionless actors depict images from the Hebrew Bible while a narrator explains them. These scenes tie Hebrew Bible stories with Christian Bible stories. The entire performance lasts about seven hours—the audience takes a break halfway through to eat a meal.

A man portrays Jesus riding a donkey in a crowd scene during the Oberammergau Passion Play in a town in southern Germany. More than 2,000 citizens of this Bavarian village participate in the centuries old play of the suffering of Christ, staged every 10 years and dating back to 1634. The village had taken a vow to perform the play in order to escape a plague that had threatened the population.

Beer for Lent

Germans have a long tradition of drinking especially strong beer during Lent. During the medieval period, German monks had to fast. They did not eat much food, but were allowed to drink beer. They began brewing special Lenten beers called *Bocks* or *Starkbier* ("strong beer"), which had a higher caloric content than ordinary beer. Depending on how the beer was brewed, it could have either a higher or lower alcohol content than ordinary beer. The *Doppelbock* made by the monks of St. Francis of Paula in Bavaria had a fairly low alcohol content and a strong, malty aroma. The monks called it "liquid bread." Today *Bock* and *Doppelbock* beers are still popular drinks during Lent, especially in Bavaria.

A man dressed in traditional Bavarian clothing drinks from a beer glass during a traditional Ash Wednesday get-together in Germany.

Lent in Ireland

In Ireland, the fourth Sunday of Lent is also Mothering Day or Mother's Day. This custom began around 1700, when people would be suffering from the deprivation of Lent and needed something to lift their spirits. Children working away from their homes would be allowed to visit their parents on this day and attend their home, or mother, church. Services centered on Mary, mother of Jesus. After services, children picked flowers for their mothers and then enjoyed a special meal together. The celebration of Mother's Day during Lent faded after the Industrial Revolution but became popular again following World War II.

Yom Kippur in Ireland

Although Ireland is one of the most Catholic countries in Europe, it also has a small but active Jewish community. The town of Cork, for example, is currently home to fewer than 100 permanent Jewish residents, most of them the descendants of Jews who fled there from Russia in the late 19th century. These Jewish residents still attend services at the local synagogue and use the Jewish cemetery as well as participate in Irish city life. The Jewish community is well connected with the world of Jews outside Cork and Ireland. Every year Jews from the United States and England visit for the High Holy Days. A group of rabbis and other Jewish leaders from London travel to Cork to help the community celebrate Yom Kippur by doing the readings, singing the Kol Nidre prayer, and performing other rituals.

Lent in Italy

During Lent Italian Catholics tend to go to church more regularly. Some particularly devout people may go to Mass every morning for the 40-day period. Even less-strict Catholics go to Mass every day during Holy Week, or every day between Palm Sunday and Easter.

A nun holds her rosary in St. Peter's Square during the Palm Sunday Mass at the Vatican.

In Italy, churches are packed on Palm Sunday. Italian churches hand out small pieces of palm leaves, sometimes wrapped in plastic. On Palm Sunday, Italian children help their parents make crosses out of palm fronds to give to friends and family. Many families save these gifts for the entire year. When a new batch of palm crosses arrives the next year, they take out the old palms and burn them or bury them. This symbolizes the destruction of last year's sins and the beginning of a new year, in which the people hope they will sin less.

The archdiocese of Milan celebrates Lent on a slightly different schedule from the rest of the Roman Catholic world. The Catholics in Milan and the surrounding area of Lombardy and part of nearby Switzerland follow the Ambrosian Rite, a special service named for St. Ambrose, the fourth-century bishop of Milan. People in this area do not begin Lent on Ash Wednesday. Instead, they celebrate Carnival for the rest of the week after Mardi Gras. They hold their largest festivities on Saturday, which is called *sabato grasso*, or "Fat Saturday." On Fat Saturday, people attend parades and festivals. Many people dress up as a character called Meneghino, a man dressed in a 3-cornered hat, red-and-white striped stockings, and an umbrella; he looks somewhat like the American George Washington, except for the stockings.

Carnival in Venice

Venice's Carnival has been notorious since the 1200s because so many people engage in wild parties.

Children especially like to eat pastries called *chiacchiere*, little strips of fried dough sprinkled in sugar that are popular on Fat Saturday. Milanese Christians begin Lent the next day. Though Lent starts on a Sunday for the Christians of this area, Holy Week and Easter fall on the same days as they do for the rest of the Roman Church, so the Milanese have a slightly shorter fast period than other Italians observing Lent.

As the end of Lent draws near, Italians start preparing for a big Easter feast. Bakers in and around Naples, Italy, begin preparing wheat pies called *pastiera*, in order to have them ready for the rush of customers on Easter. Italian families collect red onion skins and use them to dye Easter eggs, as artificial egg dyes are not popular in Italy. They boil the skins in water and vinegar, and then add the eggs. The onion skins give the eggs a reddish-brown color. These eggs are often baked into braided bread that is served on Easter.

Breaking Fast after Yom Kippur in Italy

Jews in the Piedmont region of northern Italy would sometimes break their fast with slices of toasted sweet bread sprinkled with cinnamon and sugar and soaked in red wine. In the same region, the dessert of the post-Yom Kippur meal was often a sponge cake flavored with almonds. Jews in Rome might eat a fish called red mullet cooked with raisins and pine nuts.

Charity and Lent in the Netherlands

A Dutch Christian charity called Vastenaktie has tried to encourage young Christians to treat Lent as a sort of "Christian Ramadan." Ramadan is an Islamic month in which Muslims do not eat or drink during the day. The organization laments the fact that most Dutch Christians ignore Lent's fasting rules. Although many Dutch still try to make some sacrifice or do charitable work, only a few thousand of the Netherland's 5 million Roman Catholics fast. The charity hopes that a stricter fasting practice will restore spiritual meaning to the season of Lent.

A mother's hands adjust the hood of a young penitent before he participates in a Holy Week procession in Seville, Spain. Hundreds of processions take place throughout Spain during the last week of Lent.

Holy Week in Spain

In Spain, Holy Week is called *Semana Santa*. It is the most important week of the Christian religious calendar. Towns throughout Spain hold large celebrations during this week. The festivities in the city of Seville and the entire region of Andalusia are especially elaborate. Photos of the processions have appeared around the globe, making Seville's Holy Week one of the most famous. Townspeople and tourists all come out to watch floats go by and to eat food that they buy from street vendors.

These religious floats, built and maintained by religious associations, are called *pasos*. They are elaborately decorated with sparkling gold and silver. Most *pasos* are used to carry large statues of Jesus or Mary, Jesus' virgin mother and a principal saint of Catholicism. Men called *costaleros* carry these floats through the streets, usually hidden from view by the curtains that hang from the base of each float. Far more people wish to carry the *paso* than can participate every year, as it is considered a great honor.

How Great Is the Role of *Costalero*?

In 2004 and 2005, heavy rains caused the cancellation of some processions in Seville. There were men who wept at the news, knowing they had missed their opportunity to be a *costalero*.

Costaleros carry a platform with the image of Jesus Christ during a Holy Week procession in Madrid. They must crawl out of the San Pablo Church, bringing the platform out on their knees because the main doors are not high enough.

The religious associations that sponsor the *pasos*, called *cofradías*, began in the 16th century. There are three types of *cofradías*, but only the ones known as Nazarenos (or Penitentes) take part in the Semana Santa processions. The Nazarenos wear dark robes and tall pointed hoods called *capirotes* that cover their faces. The purpose of the hoods was originally to hide the identity of the sinner seeking forgiveness. Now they are more symbolic of grief and penance. Slits cut in the pointed hoods allow the members of the *cofradía* to see where they are going. Other penitents accompany the procession, wearing hoods without points and carrying large wooden crosses.

Cheese Week in Russia

Cheese Week, also known as Butter Week, Pancake Week, or Maslenitsa, is the week before the Great Lent in the Eastern Orthodox Churches. It corresponds to the Carnival season celebrated in the Western Churches. This weeklong celebration is especially popular in Russia. During this

Women paint red spots on each other's cheeks during Maslenitsa, or Pancake Week, celebrations outside Moscow. Maslenitsa is a pagan holiday, which the Orthodox Church has accommodated as a week of feasting before Lent.

week, people eat a type of pancake called a bliny or blintz. Blinies are made with a lot of butter, eggs, and milk. They give believers a chance to indulge in these foods and use them up before the fasting of Lent begins. The weather is often still cold during this week, so people engage in winter activities such as sleigh riding or snowball fights. On the evening of Forgiveness Sunday, the day before Lent begins, people make big bonfires and throw their last blinies into them. They also go to religious services and ask that all their sins be forgiven.

A Colorful Lent in the Ukraine

During Lent, in preparation for Easter, Ukrainian Christians decorate eggs with elaborate painted patterns. These eggs are called *pysansky*. According to tradition, the women of the house made these eggs during Lent. They often did this at night after their children went to bed. Before a woman began to paint an egg, she would pray, "God help me," and ask that the person who received the egg would receive happiness and protection from harm. She would then draw patterns on the eggshell with beeswax and dip the egg in yellow dye. She would then add more wax patterns and dip the egg in other colors. The dyes could not color the shell in places where there was wax. Once the egg had been dipped in all the dye colors, the woman would melt the wax off in a candle flame, leaving behind an elaborate and colorful pattern. Some people in Ukraine still make these eggs today.

Lent in the United Kingdom

The United Kingdom includes England, Scotland, Wales, and Northern Ireland, and across its territory Lent is observed by both Church of England Protestants and Roman Catholics. In the United Kingdom, the

Giving Up the Internet

Some college students in England give up social networking Web sites such as Facebook and MySpace for Lent. They say that the sites are addictive, so giving them up is very difficult. This also helps them focus on schoolwork and seeing their friends in person. Others go even further and give up the Internet entirely.

Carnival season just before Lent is called Shrovetide because it leads up to Shrove Tuesday. Shrovetide is a more somber celebration than some carnivals, with more emphasis on confessing sins and less on parties.

Hot cross buns are a favorite Lenten tradition in the United Kingdom. They are buns made from a buttery dough flavored with cinnamon, nutmeg, and cloves, and marked with a cross shape before baking. This tradition started in 1361, when the monks of St. Albans Cathedral north of London gave out hot cross buns to the poor on Good Friday. The cross on the bread symbolizes the cross used to execute Jesus.

On Good Friday devout Christians in the United Kingdom attend church services around 3 o'clock in the afternoon, since they believe that Christ was crucified around this time. A number of superstitious beliefs are associated with Good Friday. Fishermen do not catch fish on Good Friday, and farmers

Hot cross buns, shown here, are a traditional Good Friday treat in the United Kingdom. The shape of the cross on the buns recalls the suffering of Jesus on the cross.

do not plant crops, since it is believed that iron should not enter the ground on this day. Also sailors used to take hot cross buns with them on their sailing ventures, since they believed that these buns would protect them from shipwrecks.

Miracle Bread

English legend says that bread baked on Good Friday will never get moldy.

The British clergy have attached progressive politics to religious celebrations that appeal to the secular humanism of the continent. In 2008, Anglican bishops in England called on believers to use Lent as an opportunity to improve the environment as well as their souls. The bishop of London asked his parishioners to reduce their carbon footprints (the total amounts of gas, oil, and other energy sources they used on a day-to-day basis) as a Lenten sacrifice. The bishop of Liverpool asked people to simply stop wasting energy. These bishops suggested that living a life more sensitive to the health of the planet was a better alternative to traditional Lenten sacrifices, such as giving up alcohol or chocolate, because the traditional sacrifices do not benefit the planet as a whole.

Latin America

Lent in Latin America

Roman Catholicism is the dominant religion in almost all of Latin America. The region was colonized by Spain and Portugal in the 16th and 17th centuries. Catholic missionaries quickly converted most Native Americans to their religion. Spain and Portugal were among the most devout Catholic countries in Europe even at that time, and their Latin American colonies took on their religious traditions. As a result, Lent is more energetically observed in Latin America than it is in most other parts of the world. The Native Americans of the area have incorporated their own traditions into Christian practices, so many Latin American Lenten rituals include indigenous traditions that did not come from Europe.

Using her cell phone, a young woman takes a photograph of a flower carpet being made in Antigua, Guatemala, during Palm Sunday.

Before Lent begins, many towns in Latin America celebrate Carnival. The Carnival of Rio de Janeiro in Brazil is one of the most famous, but the custom is widespread throughout South and Cen-

tral America and the Caribbean. People eat, drink, and dance to street bands. The carnivals of some countries, such as Colombia and Ecuador, incorporate old Indian customs from the festivals that Native Americans held before the arrival of the Spanish. For example, in some festivals a popular snack is the leaves of the coca plant (people chew them but do not swallow them). Coca is the source of the drug known as cocaine, but chewing coca leaves is not like taking cocaine; it gives a feeling of energy but does not have the same extreme or addictive effects as cocaine. Many Indian families raise guinea pigs to eat on special occasions, so guinea pig is now considered a festive meat (like turkey at Thanksgiving).

The festivities come to an end on Ash Wednesday. The devout go to Mass that day to repent their sins and receive a smudge of ashes on their foreheads. The less devout might go to the beach to cool down. This is a tradition in Trinidad and Tobago, which is near the Equator and always hot.

Catholics in Latin America tend to be observant of Lenten practices such as fasting and attending Mass. Many Latin Americans abstain from eating meat on Fridays during Lent.

Pilgrims walk down a street as they leave the church after performing a scene from the Bible in celebration of Palm Sunday in a Mexico City neighborhood.

Religious processions are very common in Latin America, especially on Good Friday, though they can happen any day throughout Holy Week. In many towns on Holy Thursday and Good Friday, professional actors gather to participate in the Way of the Cross. They pass through the streets of the town and reenact the Crucifixion at the end of the ceremony. In other towns, the townspeople themselves participate in religious processions.

Yom Kippur in Latin America

In the 1400s, Spanish Jews were forced to either convert to Christianity or leave the country. Many who left fled to Portugal, but soon they faced persecution there as well. Those who converted and pretended to be Christian often retained Jewish customs but had to conceal their ritual practices from outsiders in order to escape detection and possible imprisonment. During Yom Kippur, for example, Jews did not want Christians to see them fasting. They would have their servants bring them meals, and then send them away while they disposed of the food. Sometimes they would say they had no appetite, or that they were fasting in honor of Jesus' mother, the Virgin Mary. Many Jews escaped to the Americas, where they hoped to find more religious freedom, but in countries ruled by Spain and Portugal, they were subject to the same hatred they had tried to leave behind in Europe.

Today there are small communities of Jews throughout Latin America. Many larger cities have synagogues where believers can attend Yom Kippur services. Argentina has the largest Jewish population in Latin America. Most of Argentina's approximately 230,000 Jews live in and around the capital city, Buenos Aires. Jews in Argentina are allowed to take Yom Kippur as a public holiday. Many Argentine Jewish children attend Jewish schools, where they learn about their religion and how to speak and read Hebrew in addition to the usual school subjects. That way, when they attend services on holidays such as Yom Kippur, they can understand the Hebrew service.

Jews in Argentina and other parts of Latin America observe Yom Kippur by asking forgiveness of one another and eating a large meal with their families before beginning their fast. Beef is a popular meat in Argentina. Some Argentine Jews prepare for their 25-hour Yom Kippur fast by eating a big meal of steak, which can stave off hunger for hours. If there is a *mikvah* nearby, they may use it for a ritual bath, though *mikvahs* are not available in much of Latin America. Jews who live near synagogues attend services, while Jews who do not may observe Yom Kippur by fasting and praying at home.

Unique Traditions and Customs
Yom Kippur in Argentina

The Argentine town Moises Ville has a unique claim to fame: it is the home of some of the world's only Jewish cowboys, or gauchos as they are called in Argentina. The town was founded on the Argentine pampas (grassy fields in the countryside) in 1889 by eastern European Jews fleeing persecution in Europe. They built four synagogues, a theater, a Hebrew school, and a public library. They made their living herding cattle on horseback. They adopted Argentine customs such as drinking an herbal tea called *mate* and wearing baggy Argentine trousers while still keeping their Jewish traditions. They would prepare themselves for the Yom Kippur fast by eating big meals of steak, and break their fast with a mixture of European Jewish foods such as apple strudel and local Argentine fare. When believers left the synagogue after Yom Kippur evening services, they walked outside to the sound of crickets singing in the grass and cattle lowing in the fields. Today only about 10 percent of the town is Jewish, but these Jews still maintain their traditional blend of Jewish and Argentine customs.

Torch-lit Processions in Brazil

On Holy Thursday, people in Goiás, Brazil, participate in processions that reenact the arrest and crucifixion of Jesus. Men representing the Praetorian Guard, the Roman soldiers who arrested Jesus, dress in robes and wear tall cone-shaped masks with holes for their eyes and mouths. They walk through the streets carrying flaming torches, forming a torch-lit procession.

Carrying the Faith in Ecuador

In Ecuador people hold religious processions in the streets throughout Holy Week. Some of the most memorable are the Good Friday processions held in the city of Quito. Believers carry statues of Jesus and Mary through the city. As they do in the Philippines, people whip themselves and drag crosses through the streets. Some of them wear thorns on their heads or chains on their feet. Male penitents wear purple robes and hoods, because purple has long been a color associated with penitence and mourning in the Christian church. Female penitents also wear purple and cover their faces with black veils. They are called Verónicas, after the woman who wiped Jesus' face as he carried his cross. Most processions finish at 3 P.M., traditionally the hour of Jesus' death.

At 6 P.M., churches hold a ceremony commemorating Jesus' removal from the cross and his burial. Specially chosen believers remove the nails from the statue of Jesus and hand his body to a group of women who

Spring Soup

In Quito people like to eat a kind of soup called *fanesca* during Holy Week and on Fridays during Lent. This soup is made of salt codfish, vegetables, grains, cheese, and boiled eggs. Some cooks make it with 12 different kinds of beans and grains, to represent the 12 apostles. *Fanesca* is also called spring soup because it is made with vegetables first available in the spring.

place the statue in a coffin. Men called *santos varones*, or saintly men, carry the coffin through the streets to a symbolic burial site. The streets of Quito are absolutely packed for these processions, and the entire city shuts down for the day on which they take place.

Ecuadorians also love to go to the beach during Semana Santa, and popular beaches can be packed with revelers. Holy Thursday, Good Friday, and Holy Saturday are official holidays in Ecuador, but many businesses close during all of Holy Week. On Palm Sunday, Ecuador's markets are full of merchants selling palms. People buy them and weave them into ornaments such as large crosses. They take these to church and then emerge with them after Mass and wave them in the streets as they go home

Old World Traditions Live On in Guatemala

Antigua, Guatemala, is known for its elaborate celebrations during Lent and Holy Week. The town was originally colonized by missionaries from Seville, Spain, which is also known for its Holy Week festivities. Antigua's traditions began during the colonial period, but over time the town has put its own spin on the activities.

All six weeks of Lent are festive, with processions in the streets every Sunday, but the real celebration takes place during Holy Week. The entire population participates in Holy Week activities. Many people belong to religious brother- or sisterhoods (organizations or associations that exist to help their members

Spectators watch as a float with Jesus carrying the cross is carried through the streets of Antigua, Guatemala, in celebration of Palm Sunday.

show spiritual devotion) and each one is associated with a particular church. The associations arrange the many religious processions that take place during Lent and Holy Week.

During these processions, statues of Jesus and Mary are carried through the streets. These statues are one of the most unique aspects of Lent in Antigua. They were made during the time of Spanish rule and date back to the 1600s. The faithful believe that the statues themselves have spiritual power and can grant requests. These statues were important in the Spanish efforts to convert Mayan Indians to Christianity because the Maya believed the statues were variations of their own deities, possessing the same spiritual force. Each brother- and sisterhood maintains certain statues. They care for them throughout the year and present them in the Holy Week processions.

Lent in Mexico

The *Via Crucis*, or Way of the Cross, that takes place in Iztapalapa, Mexico, is one of the largest passion plays in the world. Iztapalapa is a small town that is gradually being absorbed by sprawling Mexico City. More than 1 million people come every year to watch the play. All of the townspeople put their lives on hold for a week and transform into participants in the last days of Jesus' life. There are no professional actors, sets, or stages. Instead, the locals serve as the cast and their town as the stage. Children act as villagers. The town spends months each year planning its next passion play. Townspeople strive to be given the main parts of Jesus and Mary. To be cast in one of these roles is a great honor. The part of Jesus is especially strenuous, because the actor must actually drag a 200-pound cross a great distance in the hot sun, and then be tied onto it.

On the Friday before Good Friday, many Mexicans set up altars to La Dolorosa, or Our Lady of Sorrows, in their homes. They decorate these altars with plants, flowers such as calla lilies, candles, and small statues of religious figures. Friends and relatives visit one another to admire their altars and drink fresh fruit drinks. In Oaxaca, a state in southeast Mexico, these altars often include Chia Pets, clay animal figurines that are coated

A four-year-old boy, center, carries his cross during a Good Friday procession along the streets of Mexico City. Thousands of people line the streets to watch people struggle, wearing thorned crowns and carrying crosses, up a two-mile hill in this neighborhood, to cleanse themselves of sin

with seeds. The seeds sprout into green grass shoots, thus symbolizing Jesus' resurrection.

Some neighborhoods hold larger fiestas for La Dolorosa. Street vendors sell cakes with marmalade, sweets made with coconut or tamarind, rolls filled with cheese or chicken, and fried plantains (a fruit belonging to the banana family, but not as sweet as bananas). People walk through the streets clacking wooden *matracas*, or noisemakers, to make a loud noise and enhance the festive atmosphere. On Lenten Fridays, Mexicans enjoy eating a traditional dessert called *capirotada*. This is a dish made of sliced bread rolls, butter, milk, cheese, brown sugar, raisins, tomatoes, onions, and plantains.

Oaxaca's Día de la Samaritana

The people of Oaxaca, Mexico, celebrate the festival of Día de la Samaritana on the fourth Friday of Lent. This festival commemorates Jesus' encounter with a Samaritan woman at a well. Churches, schools, and businesses hand out free ice cream and fruit drinks to passersby.

Holy Week on the Beach

Most Mexican schools close for two weeks around Holy Week. Mexicans use this opportunity to take beach vacations, and Mexican beaches can be very crowded during Holy Week.

In Mexico, Holy Week can be quite festive. In fact, the entire week can be something of a street festival. Vendors set up booths selling snacks such as cookies called *roscas*, nut bars called *muganos*, and fruit drinks called *aquas frescas* made from fresh melon and other fruits such as mangos, papayas, and guavas. They decorate these booths with flowers, paper cut into shapes, fresh fruit, and palm fronds from Palm Sunday.

On Palm Sunday, some Mexican towns put on processions reenacting Jesus' entry into Jerusalem. A man portraying Jesus rides through the streets on a donkey, and crowds of people lay palm fronds on the ground before him. Outside churches, vendors sell crosses made of woven palms. Mexicans bring palm fronds to the parish church to be blessed and then proceed through the main streets of town waving the branches.

On Holy Thursday, many Latin American churches hold foot-washing ceremonies in which the priest washes the feet of 12 believers. This helps believers remember Jesus' humility when he washed the 12 apostles' feet before the Last Supper. After the Last Supper, Jesus is said to have gone to a park called the Garden of Gethsemane to pray and prepare himself to be arrested and killed. To commemorate this event, some Mexican Catholics try to visit seven different churches as a symbolic representation of the seven periods of church history. At each church they meditate on the night of Jesus' arrest, capture, and sentence to death.

Chicken or Fish?

Not all Christians agree on religious rules. Some Mexicans, for example, believe that they are permitted to eat chicken on Fridays during Lent, while others disagree and think they should follow the rule that only allows fish on Fridays.

Yom Kippur in Mexico

Jews living or traveling in Mexico sometimes struggle to find fellow Jews with whom to celebrate Yom Kippur and other Jewish holidays. The Mexican Jewish community has long kept to itself. Mexican Jews do not necessarily tell their non-Jewish friends about their religion or religious practices. This is largely because of Mexico's history of anti-Semitism. Synagogues in Mexico City post security guards during Yom Kippur services to make sure only Jewish people genuinely interested in attending services walk in. Jews living in more remote locations such as Oaxaca, which has only a handful of Jewish inhabitants, must travel to other cities to attend Yom Kippur services or pray on their own at home.

One challenge for Jews living in Mexico is making kosher food (food that obeys Jewish laws about food) for Yom Kippur. Kosher rules prohibit mixing milk and meat, so putting cheese or sour cream on an item such as a beef taco is forbidden. Mexican Jews get around these problems by using soy cheese instead of regular cheese or beans instead of meat. Jewish cooks sometimes make their own tortillas so they can be sure they are kosher. They can then make kosher Mexican tacos, burritos, and quesadillas, topped with guacamole and black olives.

Lenten Food Trends in Venezuela and Colombia

In Venezuela and Colombia, people often eat the meat of a large rodent called a capybara on Fridays during Lent. Although capybaras are mammals, the Catholic Church long ago made a rule allowing people to eat dried capybara during Lent. The reason for this had to do with the appearance of dried capybara. Dried codfish was a common Lenten food at the time, and dried capybara resembled dried codfish. Capybara are also excellent swimmers, capable of staying underwater for long periods of time, so it was not entirely clear to 16th-century observers that they were not fish. Church leaders therefore decided that it was an acceptable Lenten food. This was a practical decision as well, because dried codfish was not readily available for Lenten meals in Latin America. People today still try to find dried capybara for their Lenten meals.

Middle East

Because the Middle East has no clear boundaries, it has several definitions. The regions that make up the Middle East span southwestern Asia, often including northeastern Africa, and consist of plains and mountains, the Dead Sea, and many rivers. This area of the world is where agriculture and the earliest identified civilization originated, along with the three major monotheistic religions of Judaism, Christianity, and Islam. Today, most of the people of the Middle East are Muslim, with Jews living primarily in Israel and small numbers of Christians living throughout the region.

Many Christians in the Middle East are not members of large branches such as Roman Catholicism or Protestantism but instead are members of smaller Christian sects. There are Syriac Christians, Melkite Christians, and Armenian Christians, all of whom follow either Catholic or Orthodox practices. For Syrian Christians Lent affords a direct connection to the story of Jonah, who helped save the city of Nineveh by getting its citizens to repent. Christian residents of contemporary Nineveh still celebrate the Lent of Jonah.

Jerusalem and Israel are extremely important places to many Christians. Jesus lived and worked in Israel and died in Jerusalem. The fact that it is possible to retrace Jesus' steps during the last week of his life makes Jerusalem a very attractive destination for devout Christians of all varieties. Thousands of Christians from all over the world travel to Jerusalem for Holy Week

every year. There they can rent white robes and wooden crosses and reenact Jesus' last walk themselves. Carrying the crosses, they retrace Jesus' route through Jerusalem's Old City, following the Via Dolorosa, or Street of Sorrows. Many of these pilgrims say that the journey enhances their faith tremendously.

Wearing a traditional prayer shawl, an Orthodox Jewish man sings a prayer while facing the Western Wall (right) on Yom Kippur. Located in the Old City of Jerusalem, the Western Wall is Judaism's holiest site.

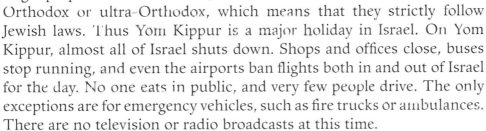

Jewish men participate in a special dawn prayer ceremony at the Western Wall in Jerusalem in preparation for Yom Kippur.

Yom Kippur in Israel

Israel is a Jewish state. About three-fourths of its population is Jewish. A large proportion of Israel's Jews are Orthodox or ultra-Orthodox, which means that they strictly follow Jewish laws. Thus Yom Kippur is a major holiday in Israel. On Yom Kippur, almost all of Israel shuts down. Shops and offices close, buses stop running, and even the airports ban flights both in and out of Israel for the day. No one eats in public, and very few people drive. The only exceptions are for emergency vehicles, such as fire trucks or ambulances. There are no television or radio broadcasts at this time.

In the days leading up to Yom Kippur, Israeli radio stations broadcast Yom Kippur prayers. Television stations run interviews with doctors who explain how to avoid discomfort while fasting. Many Israelis rush to participate in the *kapparot* ceremony, hoping to transfer their sins onto chickens. The parking lots of Jerusalem and Tel Aviv's markets are full of chicken vendors and people swinging chickens around their heads. The streets are also full of men carrying towels to the *mikvahs*, or ritual baths. Shoe stores see an increase in their sales of shoes made of cloth or plastic, as devout Jews do not wear leather shoes on Yom Kippur.

Ultra-Orthodox Jewish men wash in a *mikvah*, or ritual bath, in preparation for the Jewish holiday of Yom Kippur.

On the day before Yom Kippur begins, families have a large meal in the afternoon. This helps them build up their strength for the fast. That evening they go to the synagogue for the evening services that begin Yom Kippur, at which the cantor sings the Kol Nidre prayer. Many believers wear traditional white clothing, which symbolizes purity and forgiveness of sins. Some of them wear a white *kittel*, the robe in which dead people are buried. This symbolizes the burial of their sins and the symbolic rebirth they undergo after being forgiven.

Israeli Jews spend most of Yom Kippur in the synagogue. In Orthodox synagogues, morning services begin around 8 A.M. and continue until about 3 P.M. The congregation then goes home for a short break. People often choose to take a nap. They return two or three hours later for afternoon and evening services. After the Sun sets, the service ends with a long blast of the shofar.

Many Israeli Jews celebrate Yom Kippur as a happy, festive holiday. Rabbis tell their congregations that they should rejoice at the new opportunity God has granted them to rethink their lives and relationships. Many devout Jewish communities such as religious schools called *yeshivas* celebrate the end of Yom Kippur by singing and dancing, symbolizing the journey of their souls upward toward heaven.

Yom Kippur War

The one exception to the tradition of stopping radio and television broadcasts was in 1973, when Egypt and Syria attacked Israel by surprise on Yom Kippur. That day, the radio stations went back on the air to alert people to the danger. Ever since then, many religious and political leaders in Israel have used Yom Kippur as a day to remind people of the violence Israel has suffered and the need to end the Arab-Israeli conflict.

Children enjoy a car-free street in West Jerusalem shortly before the end of Yom Kippur, the holiest day in the Jewish year. Many residents take bicycles onto the streets as no traffic is permitted on the roads during Yom Kippur.

Nonreligious Israelis sometimes call Yom Kippur "Bicycle Day." Because almost no one drives on Yom Kippur, the city streets are completely deserted and therefore safe for bicycles. People of all ages take to the streets on bicycles, enjoying the unusual freedom to ride wherever they want. Bicycle stores are busy in the days leading up to the holiday as people purchase new bicycles or bring old ones in for repair. Nonreligious Israelis often have to work to find entertainment on a day with no television or radio and with most restaurants, movies, and other entertainment possibilities closed. Crossword puzzles and rented videos are popular options.

Lent of Jonah in Syria

The Syriac Church observes a holiday before Lent called the Lent of Jonah, also called the Fast of Nineveh. This separate Lent occurs between Epiphany (a feast at the beginning of January celebrating the revelation of Christ's divinity to the three wise men) and before the beginning of Lent. It commemorates the prophet Jonah. Jonah was ordered by God to warn the people of the city of Nineveh in Assyria (modern-day Iraq) that God would destroy their city because of their bad behavior. He boarded a ship to Tarshish to flee the responsibility of what God told him to do, and while he was on the ship, there was a storm that threatened to break it up. The sailors became convinced that Jonah was the cause of their trouble. They drew lots to see who should be cast into the pitching sea. Jonah lost but did not protest. He insisted the sailors throw him overboard in an effort to calm the weather. Jonah was then swallowed by a whale. He spent three days inside the whale, was regurgitated, and went on to warn the people of Nineveh. When they heard the warning, the people repented and fasted for three days, and God spared the city. Today believers in Syria fast for three days to mark the time Jonah spent in the whale and the fast of the people of Nineveh.

North America

Christians make up the majority of the population in North America. While Jews are a minority, they tend to be well organized and visible. Though not all Canadian and American Christians and Jews are devout or particularly observant, there are enough that Lent and Yom Kippur are noticeable events throughout the continent.

Lent in North America

About 78 percent of the residents of the United States are Christian, 52 percent of whom are Protestant. These include Episcopalians, Lutherans, Presbyterians, Methodists, Baptists, and other denominations. Evangelical Protestants make up approximately 28 percent of the U.S. population. Roman Catholics make up about one quarter of the U.S. population. Other Christian groups include Mormons, Unitarians, and Jehovah's Witnesses. About 75 percent of Canadians are Christian. About 43 percent are Roman Catholic, 24 percent are Protestant, and 2 percent are Eastern Orthodox.

Lent is a major religious ritual for many North American Christians. In a recent survey conducted by Scripps Howard News Service, about 40 percent of Americans reported that they made changes in their lives for Lent. The season is especially significant to Catholics, as about 75 percent claim to fast or otherwise change their lifestyles. Fasting is becoming common among Protestants, too. One Lenten custom common to both Canadians and Americans is keeping a dried palm frond from Palm Sunday

A woman prays with palm fronds in her hands before the start of the Palm Sunday service at St. Patrick's Cathedral in New York City.

Worshippers kneel on the sidewalk during prayers at the end of a Good Friday procession outside a Roman Catholic Church in Hartford, Connecticut.

stuck behind a mirror or headboard as a marker of the day; the leaf may stay for years. Also, though most North Americans do not mark Good Friday with public passion plays, they do organize Way of the Cross ceremonies inside their churches. Rather than parading through the streets, they will walk along the series of 14 representations on the walls of their church depicting the Stations of the Cross. At each station they will stop to meditate and pray.

Yom Kippur in North America

About 7 million Jews live in the United States, where they comprise about 2.5 percent of the population. About 350,000 Jews live in Canada. New York City, south Florida, Los Angeles, Philadelphia, and Chicago in the United States and Toronto and Montreal in Canada are home to large Jewish populations, though Jews are dispersed throughout the continent. Most Jews in North America are Ashkenazi Jews, who emigrated from Eastern and Central Europe during the 19th and 20th centuries. Some Jews have also come from the Middle East,

Passion Plays in Canada

Some organizations perform passion plays at other times of the year. The Canadian Badlands Passion Play, a large outdoor reenactment of the end of Jesus' life, takes place in July in Alberta, Canada.

St. Patrick's Day

St. Patrick's Day, the Catholic feast day honoring the patron saint of Ireland, takes place on March 17. Irish-American Catholics celebrate St. Patrick's Day by attending Mass, participating in parades, drinking beer (often dyed green), and eating corned beef. Sometimes St. Patrick's Day falls on a Friday during Lent, when Catholics are not supposed to eat red meat. Bishops get around this problem by moving St. Patrick's Day so that it falls on a day other than a Friday or to a day after Easter. Or they grant a dispensation, or give permission, to Catholics who want to eat corned beef. Usually Catholics who accept this dispensation must perform some penance or act of charity to make up for not fasting.

North Africa, and other places. North American Jews practice a wide range of traditions, from ultra-Orthodox to extremely liberal to entirely secular, or nonreligious.

The number of Jewish people in the United States who participate actively in their religion has fallen in recent years. Only about a third of the children of Jewish parents are currently raised as practicing Jews.

The shofar, an ancient Jewish ram's horn, shown here, is blown on Yom Kippur.

Synagogues

Most North American cities with some Jewish population have at least one synagogue. Every synagogue must have an interior space in which the congregation can gather to pray and listen to Torah readings. A synagogue must also include a place for the Ark of the Covenant, which contains the congregation's Torah scrolls and a *bima*, or platform for the rabbi or leader of the service to stand on while reading the Torah. In North American synagogues, the Ark and the bima are often a single structure. North American synagogues come in all sorts of styles, from traditional to very modern. Orthodox Jews in the United States and Canada require men and women to sit separately, but liberal congregations allow the sexes to sit together.

Jews have traditionally avoided trying to convert members of other faiths to Judaism, and North American Jews are still reluctant to attempt this. They are, however, trying to reach out to non-practicing Jewish people and to families of mixed faiths in an attempt to encourage Jews to come to synagogues and participate in Jewish community life. Yom Kippur is one of the days on which even nonobservant Jews participate in Jewish rituals. Synagogues typically experience their highest attendance of the year at Yom Kippur services.

Some Conservative and Orthodox Jews in North America observe the month of Elul, the month before Yom Kippur to meditate and do penance in preparation for Yom Kippur. Orthodox Jews blow the shofar after morning prayers every day during Elul.

The Day before Yom Kippur, Erev Yom Kippur, many Jews in North America try to eat a large meal to sustain them through the hours of fasting. Like Jews around the world, many Jews in North America take a ritual bath. Though there are *mikvahs* throughout the United States and Canada, not all of them are kosher, or permissible for the Orthodox to use. It is now common for Jews to use the Internet to find listings for *mikvahs* in various places.

North American Jews, like Jews around the world, begin their fast about half an hour before sunset on the day before Yom Kippur and end it after sundown the following day. Jews who observe the fast do not eat or drink anything during this time. Yom Kippur services are lengthy. There is a morning prayer service where believers pray for forgiveness. Another prayer service in the afternoon features readings from the book of Jonah, followed by services commemorating dead relatives and prayers to God to open the gates of

Yom Kippur and Baseball

In 1965, Los Angeles Dodgers pitcher Sandy Koufax refused to pitch in the first game of the World Series because it fell on Yom Kippur.

heaven. After sundown Yom Kippur ends when the shofar is blown. Many American synagogues offer attendees a light snack of dairy foods after the services.

Yom Kippur is not an official holiday in most of North America. Many Jews in the United States and Canada take the day off from work or

Closing Schools

School districts in the United States often face difficulties in deciding which religious holidays should be holidays from school. A few states consider Good Friday an official state holiday and close both schools and government offices. In most states, however, Good Friday is an ordinary day of school or work. In 2005, the school district in Hillsborough County, Florida, decided to hold school on Yom Kippur and Good Friday. Muslim parents had requested that the Islamic holiday Eid al-Fitr, celebrating the end of Ramadan, be made a school holiday. The school board decided that it would instead not recognize the Christian and Jewish holidays. After receiving thousands of e-mails, it reversed its decision and ruled that schools would close on those holidays after all. In 2006, the school board of Skokie, Illinois, also decided to hold school on Good Friday and Yom Kippur. The rationale behind this type of decision is generally that it is impossible to accommodate all religious holidays in a diverse country such as the United States, so it is best not to accommodate any particular religion.

school so that they may go to services at the synagogue and spend the day with their families. U.S. laws allow most employees to take time off for religious observances without losing their jobs, though this is not always the case.

Unique Traditions and Customs

Lent in Quebec, Canada

Historically, Lent was marked in French Canada with strict observance. Everyone over the age of 21 was expected to abstain from certain foods, such as meat, butter, and eggs, for all 40 days. Just as their ancestors did in France, French Canadians wanted to mark mid-Lent with feasting and partying, but this tradition was frowned upon.

Today, mid-Lenten celebrations are once again acceptable, and even draw tourists from other parts of the world. In the Chaudière-Appalaches region of Quebec, to the northeast of Montreal, residents of Isle-aux-Grues celebrate the middle of Lent by wearing elaborate costumes and visiting their neighbors during the day, then eating, drinking, and dancing into the night.

Passion Play in Toronto, Canada

The Toronto Passion Play is performed every year at Queensway Cathedral in Toronto. This play portrays the life, death, and resurrection of Jesus. Performances begin about a week before Easter and run through Holy Week. The last performance is on Easter Sunday. The show is about two hours long and immensely popular. The 4,000-seat auditorium is completely full for most performances.

A Monastic Lent in Kentucky, United States

Many Christians spend part of Lent at a monastery, isolating themselves to better achieve the spiritual purification they want from the season. One such monastery that offers retreat to lay guests is the Abbey of Gethsemani in Trappist, Kentucky, home to monks who live a life of silent contemplation. They open the abbey to guests who wish to come live with them and follow the daily routine of prayer, reading, and contemplation. Prayer services start at 3:15 in the morning and continue through the rosary and evening prayers at 7:30 P.M. Each visitor is given a guest room.

Trappist monks observe their first group prayer of the day called Vigils at 3:15 A.M. in Trappist, Kentucky, during the annual Lent retreat at the Abbey of Gethsemani.

Both men and women can stay as guests, though only men are allowed to enter certain parts of the monastery.

Cajun Lent in Louisiana, United States

South Louisiana has a large Catholic population, and many of these Catholics observe Lent. One of the largest and best-known pre-Lent festivals is the Mardi Gras celebrated in New Orleans, Louisiana. French and Spanish Roman Catholics colonized New Orleans, bringing with them their religious traditions. Over time, Mardi Gras has become a part of the cultural identity of the city, even for those who are not religious. There are also Mardi Gras celebrations in Mobile, Alabama, Baton Rouge, Louisiana, and other cities and towns with large Catholic populations. It is customary for restaurants in New Orleans, Baton Rouge, and other

A rider in the Krewe of Rex parade throws beads to the crowd gathered along St. Charles Avenue in New Orleans. Mardi Gras, or Fat Tuesday, is the celebration before Lent begins on Ash Wednesday.

cities in the region to offer special Good Friday menus that feature seafood dishes such as gumbo, fried shrimp, or sautéed redfish with lump crabmeat to help diners observe the fast day.

Passion Play in New Mexico, United States

In Tomé, New Mexico, the same passion play was passed down from generation to generation and performed for nearly 200 years. A local resident filmed it in 1947 and a Jesuit priest published its script in 2007. Throughout New Mexico, alarmingly realistic passion plays were once produced, in which men beat themselves raw and one actor, portraying Jesus, was literally nailed or bound to a crucifix.

Broadcasting Yom Kippur Services in North America

Synagogues in Los Angeles have begun bringing Yom Kippur services to the world through television. In 2003, the Hallmark Channel started filming and broadcasting the Yom Kippur services at the Temple of the Air as an outreach program for people confined to their homes and unable to attend services. The synagogue estimated that perhaps 1 million Jews across North America were unable to leave their homes to attend services, including a number of people in hospitals and nursing homes. The producers aimed the show at anyone who could not be in a temple praying for forgiveness, as well as any viewer who wanted to share in Jewish tradition and better understand Yom Kippur. The broadcast included a historical sketch of Yom Kippur, scenes from the Wailing Wall in Jerusalem (the most holy place in the Jewish religion), and special prayers for victims of suicide bombings.

Daytime Television and Yom Kippur

Religious services are not the only side of Yom Kippur on American television. On October 2, 2006, the soap opera *The Young and the Restless* featured a Yom Kippur story. Handsome Jewish hunk Brad was planning to celebrate Yom Kippur and wanted to atone for his sins from the previous year. He seeks forgiveness from his wife, Victoria, by apologizing to her for all the secrets that he has kept from her, in particular his affair with Sharon. After some stormy scenes with both women, he leaves to take his mother to evening Yom Kippur services.

Hasidic Celebrations in Brooklyn, United States

Brooklyn, New York, is home to a large population of Hasidic Jews. Experts estimate that perhaps 180,000 Hasidic Jews live in Brooklyn, and their population is increasing rapidly because families average 6 or 7 children. These Jews wear dark clothing and are especially observant of Jewish laws.

Many Jews feel that the act of fasting together with friends and family and then anticipating the feast to come makes Yom Kippur into something of a party. Some Jews like to prepare a treat during the day and then think about it until the Sun sets. For example, *Wall Street Journal* writer and book author Lucette Lagnado has reminisced about a ritual she and her Egyptian-born mother used to perform. They would sneak away from services during the day on Yom Kippur and prepare lemonade. They would squeeze the juice from a pile of lemons, mix it with sugar and water, and place the pitcher in the refrigerator to await sunset. They would not take even one small taste no matter how much they wanted it. Lagnado remembers the rush of finally being able to take a sip of the sweet-tart lemonade, which for her marked the end of atonement and a return to life.

Oceania

Oceania includes Australia, New Zealand, Papua New Guinea, and the many islands of the Pacific. Few Jews live in Oceania. Those that do live in small communities in Australia. There are many more Christians in Oceania than there are Jews. About two-thirds of Australians identify themselves as being Christian, although many of them do not practice any kind of religion and only about 8 percent of the population attends weekly church services. The largest Christian denominations in Australia are Roman Catholicism (26 percent) and Anglicanism (19 percent). There are also many Protestant and Eastern Orthodox Christians. New Zealand is about 15 percent Anglican, 12 percent Roman Catholic, and Papua New Guinea is 22 percent Catholic and about 5 percent Anglican. The islands of the Pacific have Catholics and Protestants scattered throughout the region. Many of the Protestants are evangelicals who do not necessarily observe Lent, but the presence of Catholics and Anglicans means that people observe Lent on many places in the islands.

Lent in Oceania

Lent in Oceania is much like Lent in Europe or North America. The devout attend church on Ash Wednesday to begin the Lenten season. They may go to confession on Shrove Tuesday in order to start Lent with a clean conscience. During Lent, people may fast by avoiding meat on Fridays, but most people do not. It is more common to try to make Lenten sacrifices such as giving up sweets.

People dressed as Roman Guards walk beside a man portraying Jesus Christ during a reenactment of Christ's crucifixion walk on the streets of Sydney, Australia, on Good Friday.

During Holy Week church attendance is higher than usual. Catholics and Anglicans may attend church on Palm Sunday to collect their palm fronds and some people save these from year to year for their spiritual value. Many people attend services on Good Friday. This is also the day when people who ordinarily do not fast are most likely to avoid eating meat. Easter services are often the most crowded services of the year. Many Christians who do not usually attend church do at least try to make it to Easter services.

Yom Kippur in Oceania

There are small communities of Jews in most of the major cities in Australia. About 110,000 Jews live in Australia, most of them Ashkenazi Jews who fled Europe during and after World War II, and their descendants. There are also about 5,000 Jews in New Zealand. A few other Jews live in the rest of Oceania, but they are few and far between.

Many of these Jews are active in their religion. Even nonobservant Jews try to attend services on Yom Kippur. It is usually not a problem for Jews to take the day off on Yom Kippur so that they may fast and attend services.

Unique Traditions and Customs
Lent in Australia

The Iona Passion Play in Queensland is one of the most famous passion plays in Australia. It was founded in Brisbane in 1958 and began touring Australia in 1961. Its script is taken from stories from all four Gospels. It has a large cast, many sets, music, and historically accurate costumes. Romans wear red capes and armor or togas (traditional Roman robes), Jewish priests wear flowing robes, and Jesus wears just a rag around his middle for the crucifixion. Actors must be sure to take off their watches and glasses before they go on stage. Part of the play's soundtrack is a version of the Stations of the Cross recorded by the Irish priest Tim Long in 1959. Most of the people who work on and act in the Iona Passion Play are nonprofessionals whose only theatrical experience is their annual participation in the play. There are a number of families who participate every year, including children, parents, and grandparents.

During the Orthodox Great Lent, the Russian Orthodox Archbishop of Sydney offers the sacrament of Holy Unction, or Anointing of the Sick,

Christians' Good Friday services at a cathedral in Melbourne, Australia.

Lent Event, Sacrifices for Charity

Australian Sarah White created a program called Lent Event to use Lent as a way of helping the world's poorest people. It tries to combine Lenten sacrifices with fundraising and spiritual enhancement. In conjunction with the Uniting Church in Australia, the organization encourages people to make a Lenten sacrifice for the full 40 days of Lent. It suggests that they give up things that cost money, such as coffees, candies, or entertainment. They should keep track of the money they save by giving up whatever they have chosen, and send that amount to Lent Event after Easter. Lent Event's Web site has resources such as prayers and meditations that participants can use to enhance their daily spiritual experience. The organization is open to contributions from anyone, Christian or non-Christian. It has so far financed projects in Papua New Guinea, Zimbabwe, India, West Timor, and Zambia, improving water systems, opening preschools, and providing small loans to people who want to start businesses.

at various parish churches. Holy Unction is a sacrament, or holy ritual, that is meant to help people heal physically and mentally. Anyone who is sick in mind or body is welcome to receive the sacrament. Even people with no obvious ailments can participate. Parishioners are required to attend confession before receiving Holy Unction so that their souls will be in a state of purity.

Some Russian Orthodox priests in Australia have suggested that Lenten fasting should include abstinence from watching television. They argue that fasting should not just involve physical acts, but spiritual acts as well. Spiritual fasting involves controlling the information that a person consumes. Television is a constant source of stimulation and can stir up emotions that a person may not want to feel during Lent. Envy, lust, and distress are all common feelings that can be aroused by television. It is not uncommon to see murders and other crimes on ordinary television programs. These priests say that this is hardly the sort of thing good Christians should be contemplating during Lent. They urge their parishioners to avoid television to keep their souls from being aroused in this way.

Yom Kippur in Australia

The ritual *mikvah* baths were difficult to find in Australia until recently. As of 2007, the city of Melbourne had three *mikvahs* with a fourth being built. There are plans to build an additional *mikvah* in Canberra, Australia's capital. Australian Jews hope this will make it easier for them to follow Jewish law about bathing before Yom Kippur.

Lent in New Zealand

Every Lent, the Caritas Aotearoa New Zealand, a Catholic agency for peace, justice, and development, conducts its Caritas Lent Appeal. From Ash Wednesday until Easter Sunday the organization tries to get Catholics to send it donations. The organization runs projects to help the poor, especially refugees, in Southeast Asia, Africa, and other places in need. It also fights for protections against child labor, access to refugees in war zones, and improved living conditions in the developing world.

On Good Friday all the shops and public establishments are closed. Prayer services are held in churches, which also include a reenactment of Jesus' journey to the place where he was crucified.

Glossary

abstain   To avoid doing something

Anti-Semitism, Anti-Semitic   Hating Jews; against the presence of Jews

apostle   One chosen and trained by Jesus in the New Testament to preach the gospel Bible collection of religious writings that are the essential texts of Christianity

Aramaic   A language spoken in the Middle East; the language that the historical Jesus spoke and the main language of the Jewish laws called the Talmud

Ashkenazi   A group of Jews descended from medieval Jews who lived around the Rhine River in Germany and then migrated to eastern Europe; European Jews

atonement   The act of making up for sins so that they may be forgiven

canon law   Church law; the laws that govern the Roman Catholic, Anglican, and Eastern Orthodox churches

cantor   A singer; a professional singer who leads religious services

confession   The act of telling another person one's sins; a sacrament in the Roman Catholic Church in which a person tells his or her sins to a priest, who then orders the person to do penance and asks God to forgive him or her

crucifix   A cross, often with a representation of Jesus affixed to it

crucifixion   The act of crucifying someone; the act that killed Jesus

day of abstinence   A day on which people are not supposed to do a certain thing, especially meaning eating

disciple   A student who follows the teachings of another; in Christianity, any of the professed followers of Christ in his lifetime

Eastern Orthodox Church   The group of Christian churches that includes the Greek Orthodox, Russian Orthodox, and several other churches led by patriarchs in Istanbul (Constantinople), Jerusalem, Antioch, and Alexandria

fast day   A day on which people are supposed to eat a limited amount of food, typically one full meal

feast day   A day on which some religious event is celebrated and believers are required not to fast; in other words, they are not allowed to fast and must eat

flagellation   The act of whipping

gospel   One of the four books (Matthew, Mark, Luke, and John) in the New Testament that describes the life and actions of Jesus

High Holy Days   The Jewish holidays of Rosh Hashanah, Yom Kippur, and the days in between

Holy Land   Israel and the area surrounding Jerusalem; the area in which Jesus lived. This land is revered by Christians, Jews, and Muslims.

Kol Nidre   The prayer recited in synagogues at the beginning of the Jewish holiday Yom Kippur

Mass   A religious service in the Christian Church, including the ceremony of the Eucharist

movable feast   A religious feast day that occurs on a different day every year

New Testament   The books of the Bible that were written after the birth of Christ

Old Testament   The Christian term for the Hebrew Scriptures of the Bible, written before the birth of Christ

Orthodox   Conforming to tradition or accepted faith. In Judaism, Orthodox Jews follow strict religious rules. In Christianity, Orthodox Christians are members of one of the Eastern Orthodox Churches.

passion   The events in Jesus' life that led up to his death, including his trial, torture, suffering, and crucifixion

penance   The repentance of sins, including confessing, expressing regret for having committed them, and doing something to earn forgiveness

Protestant   A member of a Christian denomination that does not follow the rule of the pope in Rome and is not one of the Eastern Orthodox Churches. Protestant denominations include Anglicans (Episcopalians), Lutherans, Presbyterians, Methodists, Baptists, and many others.

rabbi   A Jewish religious leader

repentance   The act of changing one's attitude and actions to gain forgiveness for a sin

Rosh Hashanah   The Jewish New Year

sacrament   A religious ritual that conveys God's blessing and helps the believer commune with God. Most Churches consider baptism and the Eucharist to be sacraments. The Roman Catholic Church includes confirmation, marriage, confession, holy orders, and anointing of the sick.

Sephardic   Originating from the group of Jews who lived in Spain during the medieval period and then moved to the Middle East after they were expelled in the late 1400s

shofar   A ram's horn used as a trumpet in Jewish rituals

Stations of the Cross   A ceremony in which believers retrace the events of Jesus' crucifixion and death

tallit   A prayer shawl worn by Jewish men during prayer services

Talmud   The document that encompasses the body of Jewish law and customs

Tishri   The seventh month of the Hebrew calendar

Torah   Jewish scriptures, the first five books of the Hebrew scriptures, which serve as the core of Jewish belief

vigil   A period in which a person stays awake to await some event

Way of the Cross   *See* Stations of the Cross

Yom Kippur   The Jewish Day of Atonement

Bibliography

∽

Agnon, Shmuel Yosef. *Days of Awe: Being a Treasury of Traditions, Legends, and Learned Commentaries concerning Rosh ha-Shanah, Yom Kippur, and the Days between, Culled from Three Hundred Volumes, Ancient and New.* New York: Schocken Books, 1965.

Goodman, Philip. *The Yom Kippur Anthology.* Philadelphia: Jewish Publication Society of America, 1992.

Greenfield, Howard. *Rosh Hashanah and Yom Kippur.* New York: Holt, Rinehart, and Winston, 1979.

Hanh, Thich Nhat. *Heart of Buddha's Teaching.* New York: Broadway Books, 1999.

Harvey, Peter. *An Introduction to Buddhism: Teachings, History, and Practices.* Cambridge: Cambridge University Press, 1990.

Heyer, Robert, ed. *Celebrating Lent.* New York: Paulist Press, 1974.

Hinson, E. Glenn. *The Church Triumphant: A History of Christianity up to 1300.* Macon, Ga.: Mercer University Press, 1995.

Johnson, Paul. *A History of Christianity.* New York: Atheneum, 1977.

Olson, Roger. *The Story of Christian Theology: Twenty Centuries of Tradition & Reform.* Downers Grove, Ill.: InterVarsity Press, 1999.

Robinson, George. *Essential Judaism: A Complete Guide to Beliefs, Customs, & Rituals.* New York: Simon & Schuster, 2001.

White, Michael. *From Jesus to Christianity: How Four Generations of Visionaries and Storytellers Created the New Testament and Christian Faith.* San Francisco: HarperSanFrancisco, 2004.

Wilson, Brian. *Christianity.* Upper Saddle River, N.J.: Prentice-Hall, 1999.

Further Resources

Books

The Last Week: A Day-by-Day Account of Jesus' Final Week in Jerusalem. By Marcus J. Borg and John Dominic Crossan. Published in 2006 by Harper One, San Francisco. A historical analysis of the events in the Gospel of Mark.

The Book of Jewish Practice. By Louis Jacobs. Published in 1987 by Behrman House, West Orange, N.J. A comprehensive guide to the history, development, and application of various Jewish rituals and customs.

Lent, Holy Week, and Easter: A Ceremonial Guide. By Leonel L. Mitchell. Published in 1996 by Cowley Publications, Cambridge, Mass. A guide to the liturgies and spiritual meanings of Easter as they pertain to the Western Church.

The Week of Salvation: History and Traditions of Holy Week. By James Monti. Published in 1993 by Our Sunday Visitor, Huntington, Ind. An in-depth study of the liturgical and devotional practices of both Western and Eastern Churches during Holy Week.

Rosh Hashanah and Yom Kippur. By Mirian Schlein. Published in 1983 by Behman House, New York. A description of the High Holy Days.

Celebrating the Jewish Year: The Fall Holidays. By Paul Steinberg. Published in 2007 by the Jewish Publication Society of America, Philadelphia, Pa. Covers the historical origins, rituals, and customs of the High Holy Days, including contemporary perspectives.

Palm Sunday and Holy Week Services. By Robin Knowles Wallace. Published in 2006 by Abingdon Press, Nashville, Tenn. A guide to the religious services held during Holy Week.

Web Sites

Chabad.org. http://www.chabad.org. A Web site with extensive information on Jewish theology and customs.

"Christian History Corner: Why does Easter's date wander?" http://www.christianitytoday.com/ct/2004/aprilweb-only/4-5-42.0.html. This article explains the scheduling of Easter.

The Ethiopian Orthodox Tewahedo Church Faith and Order. http://ethiopianorthodox.org/english/indexenglish.html. This Web site has information on Lenten practices in the Ethiopian Orthodox Church.

Greek Orthodox Archdioceses of America. http://www.goarch.org/en/ourfaith. Visit this Web site to learn about the Greek Orthodox faith.

Islam Online. http://www.islamonline.net/servlet/Satellite?c=Article_C&cid=120 1957837897&pagename=Zone-English-News/NWELayout. An article on Lent as the "Christian Ramadan."

The Sino-Judaic Institute. http://www.sino-judaic.org. Visit this Web site to learn about the Jews of China.

Stations of the Cross. http://www.cptryon.org/prayer/child/stations/index.html. This is an interactive, easy-to-follow guide to the Stations of the Cross and how they may pertain to one's day-to-day life.

The Toronto Passion Play. http://www.torontopassionplay.com. This Web site contains information about the history and details of the passion play performed annually at Queensway Cathedral in Toronto, Ontario.

The Union for Reform Judaism. http://www.urj.org. This Cleveland, Ohio-based organization has been a leading voice of progressive Judaism in the United States since 1873. Its 900 member congregations have more than 1.5 million members, a majority of the U.S. Jewish population.

Picture Credits

Index

૭௨

Page numbers in *italic* indicate illustrations.

Great and Holy Week, 15–19
Great Lent, 12, 14, *21*, 45, 70, 99
Guatemala, *74 79*, 79–80

H

hard-boiled eggs, 10
Haredi, 30
Hasidic Jews, 97
Hebrew traditions, 25–28, 31, *40*, 48, 64, 77
High Holy Days, 28, *32*, 32, 66, 103
Holy Land. *See* Israel
Holy Monday, 15, 58
Holy Saturday, 7, 15, 19, 50, 62, 76, 79
Holy Thursday. *See* Maundy Thursday
Holy Tuesday, 15
Holy Unction, 99, 101
Holy Wednesday, 15
Holy Week, 7, 15–19. *See also*
    Great and Holy Week
    in Ecuador, 78–79
    in Europe, 61–62
    in Latin America, 75–76
    in Mexico, 82
    in Spain, *69*, 69–70, *70*
honey, 32, 63, 64
hospitality, 18, 31, 39
hot cross buns, 72, 72–73

I

India, *24*, 54
Internet, during Lent, 72
Ireland, 66
Islam, 24, *51, 52*
Israel, *2, 85*, 85–87, *87*
Italy, 61, 66–68, *67*

J

Japan, 35, 49, 54
Jesus Christ, 5, 8, 14, 16–17, 43, 45–46, 47, 48,
    50, 53, *57, 58*, 58, 62, 64, *65*, 66, 69, *70*,
    72, 76, 78–82, 84, 90, 94, 96, *98*, 99, 102
Judaism. *See* Ashkenazi Jews; Bene
    Israel Jews; Hasidic Jews; Israel;
    Orthodox Jews; Sephardic Jews;
    Ultra-Orthodox Jews; Yom Kippur

K

kapparot, *29*, 29–30, 44, 63, 85
Kol Nidre, 31–32, 63, 86, 104
kosher, 30, 83, 92

L

Laos, *33*, 54–55
Last Supper, 18, 82

Latin America, 74–83
Lent, 3, 4–23. *See also* Great Lent
    in Africa, 42–43
    in Asia, 49–50
    in Australia, 99, *100*, 101
    in Cameroon, 45
    in Chad, 45
    in Egypt, 45
    in Europe, 61–62
    in Guatemala, *74, 79*, 79–80
    in Ireland, 66
    in Italy, 66–68, *67*
    in Latin America, 74–76
    in Lesotho, 47
    in Mexico, *75, 81*, 80–82
    in the Netherlands, 68
    in Nigeria, 48
    in North America, *89*, 89–90,
        90, 94–96, *95, 96*
    in Oceania, 98–99
    in Philippines, 56–58, *56, 58*
    in Senegal, 48
    in Spain, *69*, 69–70, *70*
    in Thailand, 58
    in Uganda, 48
    in Ukraine, 71
    in the United Kingdom, 71–73
    in Vietnam, 60
Lenten Sundays, 13, 22
Lent of Jonah, 88
Lesotho, 47
Luther, Martin, 5–6

M

Mahayana Buddhism, 35
Mardi Gras, 10, *11*, 67, 95, *96*
Maslenitsa, *62, 70, 71*
Mass, *4*, 46, *50*, 61, 62, 66, *67*, 75, 79, 91, 104
Maundy Thursday, 15, 18–19, *56*, 78
Mexico, *75*, 80–83, *81*
Middle East, 84–88
mikvah, 26–27, 30, 31, 63, 64, *85*, 85, 102
Moriones Festival, 23, 57–58, *58*
Moses, 24, 26
Mozambique, 47
Muslims, 3, 26, 44, 45, 48, *51*, 51,
    52, 52, 54, 68, 84, 93
Myanmar, *55*, 55

N

Netherlands, 68
New Zealand, 102
Nigeria, 48
Nineveh, 23, 84, 88
North America, *89*, 89–97, *90, 95, 96*